HONEY
& JAM

HONEY
& JAM

Seasonal Baking
from My Kitchen in
the Mountains

HANNAH QUEEN

Stewart, Tabori & Chang | New York

Published in 2015 by Stewart, Tabori & Chang

An imprint of ABRAMS

Text and photographs copyright © 2015 Hannah Queen

Library of Congress Control Number: 2014942975

ISBN: 978-1-61769-091-4

EDITOR: Camaren Subhiyah

DESIGNER: Laura Palese

PRODUCTION MANAGER: True Sims

The text of this book was composed in Enlow, Acie, Balfrey,
Bullshorn, and ITC Century.

Printed and bound in the United States

10 9 8 7 6 5 4 3 2 1

Stewart, Tabori & Chang books are available at special discounts
when purchased in quantity for premiums and promotions as well as
fundraising or educational use. Special editions can also be created
to specification. For details, contact specialsales@abramsbooks.com
or the address at right.

ABRAMS
THE ART OF BOOKS SINCE 1949
115 West 18th Street
New York, NY 10011
www.abramsbooks.com

FOR MY FAMILY

CONTENTS

A NOTE FROM MY KITCHEN

⸺ ⋟•⋞ ⸺

I was born and raised in a little house surrounded by old hemlock trees and blackberry brambles in Blue Ridge, Georgia. Set against the foothills of the Appalachian Mountains, our town is edged with rolling fields and dense green forests. The woods have an ancient feel about them, and I've spent hours berry picking, daydreaming, and driving aimlessly on back roads passing old cabins and barns.

Growing up in our small town, I didn't have access to fancy food of any sort—just simple home cooking. I remember helping my mom in the kitchen as a kid, making sweet potato casserole at Thanksgiving and cookies at Christmas, but it wasn't until my late teens that I really became interested in teaching myself to bake.

That's when I picked up my first cookbook. I tried baking orange-chocolate cupcakes, and they were so bad! I misread the instructions and added a tablespoon of orange extract instead of a teaspoon. But I kept baking and eventually made nearly every recipe in that book. I taught myself how to cream butter and sugar, make piecrust, and whip egg whites. The processes of measuring flour, whisking eggs, rolling out dough—all the components of baking—began to feel natural to me. But they were also magical. Baking felt like alchemy: combining simple ingredients to create something incredible, something that had the power to evoke feelings of home in, and bring joy to, others.

As I found my footing in the kitchen, I started seeking out new flavors, inspired by the things growing around me. How could I incorporate the taste of spring honeysuckle into a cake?

Blackberries from the woods beside my house? Wild muscadines with their vines tangled in the pine trees? I began creating recipes to reflect the bounty surrounding my home.

With my sister and mom in tow, I brought my desserts to a little stand at the Blue Ridge farmers' market. My sister and I would spend each Friday baking in our tiny kitchen, singing along to the Avett Brothers and whipping up treats like sweet potato bread, chocolate chip cookies, and blackberry cakes. Our mom would wake up with us at dawn, load up my car, and get us to the market at six A.M. to set up the stand. It was a family affair.

There's a great sense of community that comes with small-town farmers' markets. Ours is eccentric, made up of local farmers who've been at it all their lives, newcomers with small organic farms, older ladies who paint gourds in their spare time, and a guy who makes tin-can robots. You get to know the people around you, hear about their lives and how their crops are doing, pet their dogs. We'd have regulars who'd come each week—early, before the crowds—to make sure they got their favorite spiced molasses cookies.

Encouraged by the response I was getting at the market, I started taking pictures of my desserts and posting them online. I experimented with recipes and asked for feedback. I captured my favorite places in Blue Ridge and shared them on my blog, *Honey & Jam.* And people were interested. And so what started as a failed attempt at orange-chocolate cupcakes ended with a new direction for my life. I had found my calling.

Cooking and baking align you to the rhythm of the seasons, and I wanted to organize this book to reflect the natural progression of how I bake through the year. Peaches taste best in deep summer, strawberries at the start of spring, and apples in the autumn. When you find yourself craving the best of each flavor, you use what's freshest at the time. This connects you to your surroundings and the folks who grow your food. It's the best way to support your local farmers.

I am so proud to share Blue Ridge with you through these recipes. I hope this book inspires you to explore the world around you and test out your new discoveries in the kitchen.

SEASONAL BAKING

THE FARM-TO-TABLE ETHOS HAS ALMOST BECOME second nature to responsible restaurateurs and home cooks with the time and means to eat locally. We head to the farmers' market every weekend; we purchase farm shares to support local agriculture; we buy locally raised meats; we know to either gorge on tomatoes in August or put them up in jars to use throughout the year when they're not in season. Whether you're cooking savory meals or preparing desserts, food should be thoughtfully sourced. All of the cakes, doughnuts, trifles, and other desserts found in this book are meant to be baked seasonally.

Following is a guide to seasonal produce—the fruits, vegetables, and herbs used in my baking: where and when to look for them, how to choose the best, and how to store them so you get the most out of your ingredients.

SPRING

STRAWBERRIES

Strawberries are in season starting in late April or May in most parts of the country and nearly year-round in California and Florida, where most supermarket strawberries come from. While they're now ubiquitous regardless of season, strawberries are one of those fruits best obtained by picking them yourself—or at least by buying them from a local source. You can't drive far in most parts of the country without running into a small-scale strawberry farm, and there's probably one near enough that you can visit several times over the course of the season. Perfectly ripe strawberries are so delicate that commercial operations don't ship perfectly ripe strawberries. Since they don't ripen any further after they've been picked, supermarket strawberries tend to be underripe, too firm and/or rubbery, and not nearly as sweet as local berries.

⋇ STORAGE ⋇

Quite simply, *don't* store them unless you're making preserves or freezing them whole or sliced for later use in smoothies or sauces or jams. Refrigeration can make strawberries rubbery, so just keep them at room temperature and use them by the end of the day. If you must keep them longer than a day, put them in a sealed plastic bag lined with paper towels and refrigerate them. Wash strawberries just before using them (don't store them after washing, as the excess moisture encourages decay) and remove the green hulls and stems after washing so the flesh doesn't absorb too much of the rinse water.

RHUBARB

Rhubarb is one of the first signs that you've left winter behind, and one of the few fruits (technically a vegetable, but usually treated as a fruit) that actually does ripen in astronomical spring. The glorious streaky red, pink, and red-green stalks show up in cold-climate farmers' markets and in better grocers starting in early April, and in some parts of the country, the season goes through early July. (Greenhouse-grown rhubarb shows up in grocery stores year-round, but it's likely to be wan and limp, simply because turnover tends to be slower when there aren't local fresh strawberries—the classic partner of rhubarb—also available.) Choose very firm, crisp stalks and avoid any that are bendy or dried-out looking. The color can range from mostly green and white with a little pink to bright fuchsia to deep burgundy.

If there are any leaves or parts of leaves attached, remove and discard them before using the stalks, as the leaves are toxic. Wash the stalks well before using them, but don't peel them—they break down so much as they cook that the structure of the somewhat more fibrous outer layers is welcome.

⋇ STORAGE ⋇

Rhubarb will keep fairly well for about a week in an unsealed plastic bag or other container in the refrigerator crisper drawer. It also freezes beautifully, so while it's in season and plentiful, chop it into pieces, put it in zip-tight plastic freezer bags, and freeze for up to six months.

CHERRIES

I turn to sweet cherries like Bing and Rainier when they're to be paired with dark chocolate, whose pleasant bitterness is mellowed and smoothed out by the sweet fruit. They are in season from late spring through August. They can be found in grocery stores all over the country, of course, but the ones you buy locally will be sweeter, fresher-tasting, and plumper, so it's worth seeking out a small-scale grower near you.

Sour cherries—tender, juicy, almost translucent bright red "pie cherries"—are the unsung heroes of the dessert world. Their distinctive tartness offsets the sugar in sweets like pies, cobblers, cakes, and pastries in which sweet cherries would be bland or cloying. Sour cherries are in season only for a couple weeks in midsummer and aren't readily available in supermarkets, so when you see them, snag them. Try your luck at farmers' markets or Middle Eastern markets, or find a pick-your-own orchard and bring them home by the bucketful to pit and preserve or freeze for later.

STORAGE

Use cherries—especially sour cherries—as soon as you can after picking or buying them; if you must keep them for more than a day, put them in a paper bag or unsealed plastic container in the refrigerator. Rinse the cherries, pull the stems off, and pit them just before using or freezing them in airtight containers or zip-tight freezer bags.

SUMMER

RASPBERRIES, BLACKBERRIES & BOYSENBERRIES

Raspberries are the royalty of the fruit world: fragile, bursting with juice, fragrant, and more sweet than tart. The main challenge of baking with them is to keep from eating your entire stash straight out of hand before you get to the baking. Blackberries, whether they're one of the huge cultivated varieties or smaller wild ones, are the bramble berries of the people: usually fairly tart, seedier than raspberries (not that there's anything wrong with that), with a deeper fruit fragrance.

The boysenberry is actually a hybrid cross between a raspberry, blackberry, and loganberry that was probably developed in the early twentieth century in California (by a grower named Rudolph Boysen). Boysenberries look like small-lobed, elongated blackberries, and when perfectly ripe and literally bursting with juice, they're remarkably sweet, with just enough tartness to offset the sugar.

Raspberries and blackberries ripen in mid to late summer and, because they're so delicate and prone to spoilage, it makes most sense to either pick your own or buy them from a local source. They can also be quite expensive in grocery stores, even at the height of the season. Boysenberries have a shorter season, from about late May to early July, and you probably won't find them in grocery stores at all. Look for boysenberries in farmers' markets, cultivate a relationship with someone who grows them, or plant some brambles yourself.

STORAGE

Bramble berries do not keep or travel well, so use them as soon as you can after getting them into your kitchen. Keep them in shallow unsealed containers or paper bags lined with paper towels in the refrigerator—don't pile them too deep or the bottom ones will get crushed under the weight of the others. They'll keep only for one to two days. The juices tend to seep out of the thin skins at the slightest provocation, so be gentle with them, handling them only as much as is absolutely necessary; rinse them briefly just before using and pat them dry or let them air-dry.

BLUEBERRIES & HUCKLEBERRIES

There are two basic kinds of blueberries: high bush and low bush, which, as you'd imagine, describe the plants themselves. Cultivated blueberries are generally in the high bush (or half-high) category, and the berries are large, plump, and sweet, if sometimes a bit wan. Wild blueberries, native to the northeastern United States, are low bush—almost groundcovers—and produce small, firm, sweet-tart berries with exceptional flavor. Huckleberries are essentially the wild blueberries of the Pacific Northwest; they're in season from mid-August to mid-September. There are several varieties of huckleberry—deep red or dark purple, small or large, occurring in clusters or singly on the stems of the bushy plants—but the sweetest and most desirable are the larger, dark purple thin-leaf huckleberries. Some gardeners have had success transplanting wild huckleberry bushes, but for the most part, they're foraged. Go out and pick them yourself (check the USDA/Forest Service website for information about harvesting wild berries in national forests—there are rules about how many you can extract without a permit) or buy them at farmers' markets or roadside stands.

As with all berries, blueberries and huckleberries should be deeply colored—with no green or white areas remaining—when perfectly ripe. Usually the berries will release from the plant easily when they're ready; if it's hard to pull one off when you're picking, leave it and move on. If you're buying berries, check the container to make sure there are no crushed berries at the bottom.

STORAGE

Blueberries and huckleberries won't last long after picking. Keep them refrigerated in a paper bag or a shallow, loosely covered container lined with a paper towel, and don't pile them more than a few layers deep to avoid crushing the ones on the bottom. They'll last in the refrigerator for about two days. Rinse them gently just before using.

PLUMS

There are hundreds of types of plums, and any of the sweeter dessert plums will work wonderfully in these recipes. They ripen at different times throughout the summer—some as early as May, some as late as October.

Look for bright color in the skin, whether yellow, orange, red, dark purple, or green (in the case of greengage plums), with a slight softness at the stem and blossom ends. Most varieties of plums will sport a faint white coating of wax that forms naturally as the fruit ripens. If it's still present (it'll be most apparent on dark-skinned plums), it's a sign that the fruit has been minimally handled; the bloom rinses off easily. Some will be tarter than others, and if you're buying them at a supermarket—where you won't necessarily be able to ask the grower about them—the best way to determine what you're getting is to smell the blossom end, which should have a strong fruity aroma; better yet, buy one and taste it before filling your basket.

STORAGE

Plums will ripen and soften off the tree, though they won't sweeten considerably. If yours are still quite firm when you get them home, keep them at room temperature in a bowl so they get plenty of air circulation, or in an open paper bag. Once they're ripe, they can be refrigerated in a paper bag for several days. Rinse them just before using; there's no need to peel them.

PEACHES & NECTARINES

You might be surprised to learn that aside from the fact that peaches have fuzzy skins and nectarines smooth, there's no substantive difference between them. Just one gene separates them, and if you plant a peach seed, a nectarine tree may well grow from it (and vice versa). When used in desserts, peaches are often peeled; there's no need to peel nectarines, which gives them a slight advantage, convenience-wise. In late summer it's possible to find good peaches and nectarines at grocery stores, especially those that offer locally grown fruit. (I'm lucky enough to live in a part of the country where people know their stone fruit and demand the best from the produce managers at their everyday supermarkets.) Your best bet, though, is to go straight to the source, either a you-pick orchard or a farmers' market. Commercial growers have been conditioned over the years to a marketplace that rewards looks over flavor (hence the prevalence of firm, crisp fruit and the early-forming red tinge seen in the skin of modern peach varieties, which obscures the background color that would indicate

ripeness) and sweetness over balance (without a tart component, extra-sweet supermarket peaches can lack complexity and interest).

Entire books have been written about how to choose the best peaches and nectarines, but here are a few tips for picking these fruits at farmers' markets or off the tree:

- Don't be deterred by a few blemishes or bruises, but beware of broken skin (or at least resolve to use those fruits immediately, as they'll spoil quickly).

- They should be intensely aromatic—if the fruit is ripe and soft but you can't smell it from several yards away, consider taking a pass.

- Peach and nectarine varieties each have quite short seasons within a longer period from early summer to early fall, and growers usually diversify their crops to expand production time. According to fruit guru David Karp, later-ripening varieties tend to yield the best fruit: Longer maturation times allow for more sugar development and depth of flavor.

⊰ STORAGE ⊱

Firm, underripe peaches and nectarines should never be refrigerated—the cold will make the flesh mealy and prevent ripening. Keep them at room temperature in a shallow bowl until they've softened; this might take a few days. After that, they can be put in a plastic bag or other container and refrigerated for a couple days. Rinse just before using, and refrain from cutting them until the last minute, as the flesh will start to brown with exposure to air. To peel peaches, bring a large pot of water to a boil and drop them in. Cook for 30 seconds to 1 minute, then transfer them to a bowl of ice water to cool quickly and slip off the peels. If you've gotten a batch that doesn't peel easily, or that were underripe when you blanched them, either leave the peel on or use a sharp paring knife or serrated vegetable peeler.

USING YOUR REFRIGERATOR DRAWERS

Your refrigerator probably has one or two drawers at the bottom of the main chamber, maybe with little fruit and vegetable icons on them. And if yours is a newer model, each drawer probably also has a sliding lever indicating high or low humidity. Here's a good rule of thumb for using those drawers and levers to their best advantage: Set one drawer for high humidity and one for low humidity. Put produce that wilts in the high-humidity drawer and produce that rots in the low-humidity drawer. Also, put vegetables that don't emit ethylene gas in the high-humidity drawer.

HIGH HUMIDITY/ NOT ETHYLENE PRODUCING:	LOW HUMIDITY/ ETHYLENE PRODUCING:
• Dark greens	• Apples
• Lettuces	• Pears
• Fresh herbs	• Grapes
• Scallions	• Summer squash
• Cabbage family (broccoli, cauliflower, etc)	• Tomatoes
	• Citrus

APRICOTS

Apricots, which ripen in early to midsummer, are one of the trickiest fruits to pick. Almost all the apricots sold in the United States are grown in California (the trees need a warm, dry climate, but its early-spring blossoms are susceptible to frost), which means that unless you live in California, most of what you'll find in grocery stores will have been shipped while underripe. Apricots will ripen and soften after they've been picked, but they won't become sweeter, so often the supermarket specimens will ripen just fine but taste bland. Visit a pick-your-own orchard so you can select tree-ripened apricots yourself, or seek them out at farmers' markets.

Most of the apricots sold fresh commercially are Patterson apricots, which travel well but aren't incredibly appealing. Probably the best variety of apricot is the older heirloom Blenheim or Royal apricot, which is the kind that's often dried because it's so sweet, fragrant, and intensely flavorful. Fresh Blenheim apricots are rare finds—and the best place to grow them in California happens to overlap with high-rent Silicon Valley—but they are becoming more readily available in farmers' markets in the western United States. Start looking for them in late June.

Apricots should have a deep orange color, and ripe ones will be soft but not mushy and will smell fruity. Avoid apricots with green areas, as they likely won't ripen further after picking.

⚹ STORAGE ⚹

Store unripe (firm) apricots at room temperature in a bowl that allows plenty of air circulation, and they should ripen in a few days; to speed up the process, put them in a loosely closed paper bag. Ripe apricots can be kept in the refrigerator for about a week. Rinse them just before using; there's no need to peel them.

TOMATOES

Tomatoes have a long history of being used in dessert contexts—from sweet tomato jams to green tomato pies studded with raisins and nuts. There's no real trick to finding the most flavorful summer-ripe tomatoes: Whether they're heirlooms or hybrid varieties, and whatever color they are, they should smell like tomatoes, the skin should be bright and vibrant-looking (healed cracks and deformations are generally fine as long as the skin isn't broken, which makes them subject to quick decay), and they should be heavy and not too firm. Your garden, your neighbor's garden, and the farmers' market are the best places to find the most excellent specimens, probably in that order. Some growers will have greenhouse-grown tomatoes outside the height of the mid- to late-summer season, but in my experience, these aren't quite as intense in flavor as field-grown fruit (yes, tomatoes are fruits). Green tomatoes can be found in many markets year-round but are for the most part a late-summer, early-fall crop: They're the tomatoes that are picked green because they won't have time to ripen before the weather turns cold and freezes the plants.

⚹ STORAGE ⚹

Keep ripe tomatoes at room temperature and don't refrigerate them unless you have a cut one you haven't used up. They taste best if they've ripened on the vine, but if you've got a few that are green or not quite ripe, put them in a single layer in a paper bag, and if they're completely green, add an apple or banana to the bag, as it will release ethylene gas and speed the process. Green tomatoes should be full size and quite firm; they can be stored in the refrigerator in a loosely closed plastic bag.

ZUCCHINI & SUMMER SQUASH

While zucchini has long been a quick bread staple, it and its yellow squash cousins are still underappreciated in the dessert world. It's true that out-of-season grocery-store zucchini has little use in sweet treats apart from its role as a bland filler (or spice and sugar delivery vehicle) in zucchini bread, but good zucchini and summer squash, matured in the heat of mid and late summer by a local farmer or gardener, can do so much more for your baked goods. Varieties that are bred for flavor rather than for their transport or keeping properties are sweeter, with an almost floral fragrance that lends itself well to dessert making. Try them in cakes that will allow their flavor to shine through, and you won't be disappointed.

There are no hard-and-fast rules for choosing a dessert-worthy zucchini or summer squash. Good zucchini come in a variety of shades of green, from dark forest green all over to light green and white striped or spotted. Yellow squash of the best quality could be pale yellow or almost orange, and many farmers will grow several varieties. Your best bet is to head to a farmers' market and start asking questions. Most farmers will be able to point you to the sweetest and most flavorful specimens. Look for shiny, bright skin with few blemishes. Choose zucchini and squash that are firm and not at all soft or bendable and that show no signs of shriveling or drying.

⚞ STORAGE ⚟

Handle squash gently to keep from breaking the often-delicate skin and inviting deterioration. Keep zucchini and summer squash in a zip-tight plastic bag or other container in the refrigerator, preferably in the crisper drawer, for up to five days. Wash them well just before using.

FRUITS THAT RIPEN AFTER HARVEST

Some fruits and vegetables are climacteric, which means they will continue to ripen (though not necessarily become sweeter) after they've been picked from the tree, bush, or vine. They include:

• Apples	• Pears
• Apricots	• Persimmons
• Peaches	• Plums
• Nectarines	• Tomatoes

These can all be picked while still underripe, as long as they're mature, full size, and not too green. They can be ripened at home, at room temperature, in a shallow container that allows air to circulate around them (a colander works well). To speed the process, put the fruit in a loosely closed paper bag to trap the ethylene gas the fruit gives off; the gas encourages ripening.

Figs are technically climacteric, but ripening them off the tree is hit-or-miss. They should be picked as close to completely ripe, as soft as possible.

CARROTS

Carrots are widely available year-round and can be stored seemingly forever in the crisper drawer or root cellar, but they're at their sweetest and most flavorful right after they're harvested. Carrot season (yes, there is a carrot season) is late summer and early fall for mature carrots and late spring into summer for true baby carrots. Look for unusual varieties in good grocery stores and farmers' markets, and choose ones with darker coloring for more flavor—why not use deep purple carrots in your cake?

If the green tops are still attached, the foliage should be bright and fresh-looking, not wilted. The roots themselves should be firm and crisp, not pliable. Minor blemishes and imperfections are fine.

STORAGE

Remove the green tops, if any, and put the carrots in a loosely closed plastic bag; store in the refrigerator crisper drawer for several weeks. Scrub and peel them just before using.

CORN

Stop at a roadside farm stand in late summer just about anywhere in the country and odds are you'll get into a conversation—with the farmer or with other customers—about what makes a good ear of corn. Some prefer the supersweet modern hybrids with almost absurdly cloying names like Peaches and Cream, Ambrosia, and Kandy Korn. Some go for the ones that feature a more traditional corn flavor, while still being quite sweet, like the classic Silver Queen. For our dessert-baking purposes, any sweet, tender variety will work well. Definitely seek it out in summer at farmers' markets or roadside stands— corn out of season has likely been traveling for days, the sugar content falling all the while.

Inspect each cob, making sure the husks aren't too loose or dried out, and pulling back the husks at the top of the cob to see that the kernels are well formed and plump.

STORAGE

Store the ears still in their husks in a zip-tight plastic bag or other container in the refrigerator for no more than three days. Corn freezes very well: Blanch the whole cobs in boiling water for 2 to 3 minutes, transfer them to ice water to cool, then cut off the kernels and freeze in freezer-safe containers or zip-tight plastic freezer bags for up to a year.

BEETS

For some reason, beets, though they're the sweetest of all vegetables, are rarely used in desserts, an oversight I hope to correct here. They have a distinctive earthy, minerally flavor that subtly highlights dark chocolate. In late summer, farmers will be pulling the first mature beets from the ground, and this is the time to enjoy them at their best. Supermarket beets are fine, but they might have been in storage for a while; if you spy fresh beets at a farmers' market, snatch them up. Use the roots in a cake and save the tops to sauté with garlic and olive oil as a quick side dish.

Beets are best purchased with the green tops still attached and still bright green and unwilted, which means they're freshly dug. The roots should have a deep burgundy color and no blemishes and the long taproot at the end should still be present.

STORAGE

Remove the tops to keep them from drawing moisture from the roots and store tops and roots separately in zip-tight plastic bags or sealed containers in the refrigerator. Use the tops within a couple days; the roots will keep for up to two weeks. Peel them just before using.

FALL

APPLES

You really can't say you're living a full life unless, when you encounter a variety of apple you've never seen before, you pick it up and try it. In farmers' markets across the country, from August through October, people are rediscovering the beauty of . . . well, ugly apples, much as in recent years misshapen, homely tomatoes have gained favor with consumers who value flavor over appearance. True, in supermarkets Red Delicious still reigns supreme, but even there you'll likely have many more options than you would have just a few years ago. There's no way I can tell you what the best apple for eating out of hand is. You might like the deep, tart-sweet flavor of a crunchy Winesap or Arkansas Black; you might prefer the tender snap of the ultrasweet Honeycrisp; you might enjoy the mild, unassuming sweetness of a Fuji; you might even get your kicks with a puckery-tart Granny Smith or the astringent Mutsu. Any of these are great baking apples: They'll hold their shape and contribute distinctive flavor, whether sweet, tart, floral, spicy, or otherwise, to your cake or pie. The only apples you should steer clear of when baking—other than Red Delicious, which has little to recommend it apart from its classic-apple aesthetic—are those that readily break down when cooked (use them for applesauce instead); these include McIntosh, Empire, Rome, and Cortland apples.

Because apple cultivars vary so greatly, there are no hard-and-fast rules for picking ones you're sure to like other than trial and error. Ask the growers for a taste, or at least a verbal description of what their apples taste like and how they respond to cooking. Blemishes are fine, but unless you don't mind a bit of trimming and intend to use the apples right away, steer clear of fruit with bruises or soft spots or worm holes. Some people say that apples last longer off the tree if their stems are still attached, but it's debatable whether this should have much effect on your decision-making process.

STORAGE

Many apple varieties are great for long-term storage—in fact, most of the apples you see in grocery stores outside of apple season have been stored since fall. Unless you're picking your own, you probably won't be bringing home unripe apples, but if you do, leave them at room temperature for a few days before refrigerating them in a zip-tight plastic bag or other container, where ripe apples will keep for at least two weeks. For long-term storage of large quantities, wrap each apple individually in newspaper and stack them in shallow layers in boxes; keep them in a cold cellar just above freezing and they'll last for several months. Rinse apples well just before using them and wait until the last minute to peel and cut them, as the flesh will darken quickly upon exposure to air.

PUMPKINS & BUTTERNUT SQUASH

Jack-o'-lantern pumpkins are not meant to be eaten; they're bred purely for size and, aside from the seeds, they don't make good eating—the flesh is fibrous and flavorless. Sugar pumpkins, also known as pie pumpkins, on the other hand, are a different thing altogether: These small gourds—

about the diameter of a dinner plate—are grown for sweetness and feature a strong, distinctive pumpkin flavor. Butternut squash, those creamy-peach-colored hard squashes, are usually not quite as sweet, but they have a lovely dense texture that makes them excellent in desserts.

Pumpkins and butternut squash are available starting in early fall in farmers' markets and at roadside stands all over the country, and you'll find them in the produce section of any supermarket (not with the jack-o'-lantern pumpkins out front). Local growers might offer different heirloom varieties, but in most cases, a supermarket specimen will work just fine.

When buying pumpkins for cooking, be sure they're labeled "sugar" or "pie" pumpkins. The skin should be tight, smooth, and bright orange or deeper reddish orange, depending on the type, with few blemishes. They should be heavy for their size. Butternut squash should also feel heavy, which will indicate not only freshness but a smaller seed cavity and more edible flesh. If you're buying by the pound, the following trick might not matter much, but if you're buying whole squash, choose a butternut with a longer, thicker neck (at the stem end) and smaller bulb (the rounded part at the blossom end): You'll get more flesh that way, since the neck is solid and the bulb is hollow and full of seeds.

✳ STORAGE ✳

Pumpkins and butternut squash (indeed most hard winter squash) will keep for at least a month at cool room temperature. Cooked and pureed pumpkin flesh freezes very well: Put it in airtight containers or zip-tight plastic freezer bags and keep it for up to a year. Both pumpkins and butternut squash have tough skins. Either roast or steam them whole or halved and scoop the pulp from the skins, or use a vegetable peeler or sharp knife to remove the peel before you cook the flesh.

SWEET POTATOES

By state law, you can't live in Georgia if you don't adore sweet potatoes. Luckily, they're among the easiest vegetables to love. Sugary, yes, but the best will have a minerally, earthy undertone, with fruity top notes—I know it may sound like I'm talking about a top-shelf alcoholic spirit, but we do take our sweet potatoes seriously here. Excellent ones will be available in farmers' markets in mid to late fall, and you'll likely find a host of different types in a rainbow of colors, from bright purple with white flesh, to the standard orange on orange, to cream on white. Try them all to see which ones you prefer (any will work well in my cake recipes), or ask the farmers to tell you about the cultivars they're growing and why they like them. In supermarkets, you'll usually find at least two types: the regular orange Beauregard, which has a mild flavor and light texture, and the narrow, deeply colored Red Garnet or Jewel varieties, which tend to be sweeter with dense flesh.

Most sweet potatoes you'll find in markets will have been cured for a period of time after they were pulled from the ground; this means that all the scratches and minor injuries sustained as a result of spade-to-tuber contact during harvest will have dried and healed to an extent. Pass on any that have fresh gashes as well as those that appear wrinkled or withered, which indicates advanced age. Otherwise, lumpy, misshapen, and odd-looking are all fair game.

———— ❧ STORAGE ❧ ————

Sweet potatoes are easy—just keep them at cool room temperature in an open container to prevent excess moisture from forming on the surface. They'll last for at least a couple weeks. You can refrigerate sweet potatoes in a paper bag or loosely closed plastic bag if you need to keep them longer. Scrub them just before using; they do need to be peeled, either before cooking if you're chopping them first or after cooking if you're roasting or boiling them whole.

WINTER

LEMONS, ORANGES, GRAPEFRUIT & KUMQUATS

Lemons and oranges are among the most versatile and beloved ingredients in desserts, and while they're available year-round, they're at their best in winter—few scents are more evocative of the season than the spray of oil misting from an orange as you peel it.

The most common variety of lemon in grocery stores is Eureka, also called Quatre Saisons because the grafted trees produce fruit prolifically throughout the year. Meyer lemons, which have a floral aroma and are less acidic than standard lemons, are becoming more widely available in better supermarkets. They're worth seeking out during their comparatively short season, around December through May.

In my experience, the juiciest lemons are those that have smooth, thinner skin and are more spherical than oblong. If you're going to be using the zest of lemons or oranges (and you should be, or at least saving it in the freezer for later), consider choosing organically grown fruits, as the outer peel can retain pesticides even after thorough washing.

You can use any kind of orange in my recipes. Valencia oranges are grown to be good for juicing, but they don't yield the best zest or flesh. Navel oranges are ideal for eating out of hand and for the zest. Sweet, red-fleshed varieties like Cara Cara and blood oranges yield beautiful blush-colored juices.

There's little difference in flavor among types of grapefruit—pink, white, and the Texas "Ruby" varieties are all interchangeable.

Round or oval kumquats—which look like large-grape-sized oranges—are a traditional fruit used in Lunar New Year celebrations in Asia, where small potted kumquat trees are given as gifts in midwinter. They have a slightly sweet peel and very sour flesh, usually with a large seed or two that will need to be poked or squeezed out if you're using kumquats whole in a recipe.

✻ STORAGE ✻

Citrus fruits keep well in the refrigerator, best in one of the lower drawers, for several weeks. (Grapefruit can be stored at cool room temperature for about a week.) Don't store citrus in an airtight container or zip-tight plastic bag, which will promote rotting; make sure air can circulate around the fruit.

CRANBERRIES

Vaccinium macrocarpon—the standard cranberry—is grown primarily in the northeastern United States, especially in New Jersey and Massachusetts, where the particular soil and water conditions required by cranberry vines are close to ideal (commercial growers go to great lengths to reproduce those conditions elsewhere). The vines are cultivated in "bogs," glacier-formed kettle holes lined with impermeable clay and filled with layers of crushed rock, peat, and sand. Most cranberries are wet harvested in flooded bogs, but the ones sold as fresh whole cranberries (rather than as juice, canned, or as ingredients in other processed foods) are usually dry harvested. Look for them starting in mid-September and through

November. Make sure the cranberries are bright colored and firm, not soft—they should bounce when you drop them onto the counter.

Fresh cranberries will keep in an airtight container or zip-tight plastic bag in the refrigerator for at least a month; be sure to pick out any softened ones before you use them. Cranberries are easily frozen in zip-tight plastic freezer bags and can be used straight from the freezer—rinse them just before you use them.

PEARS

The most common pears are the earlier-ripening green-reddish-yellow Bartlett pears; they're juicy and soft and break down readily when cooked. Eat them raw or use them for pear sauce. Anjou pears are short-necked, green or red, firm, and sweet, perfect for poaching whole. Rust-colored Bosc, with its matte-textured skin and grainy flesh, has a pretty elongated neck and a firmness that makes it good for poaching or using in baked goods in which you want the pieces to hold their shape. Comice pears are round and green, with a smooth, firm, juicy, fine-textured flesh—great for eating raw or using in baked goods.

Look for local pears in late-summer and fall farmers' markets—even outside the major pear-producing states of Washington and Oregon, pears are relatively easy to grow. When choosing pears, don't worry about a few brown marks on the skin; as long as they're not deeply bruised, they'll be fine.

Pears are harvested from late summer to late fall, but some varieties (like Anjou, Bosc, and Comice) are good keepers and can be stored well into winter if picked when slightly unripe and kept under heavy refrigeration; in fact, these winter pears actually

benefit from spending at least a few weeks in storage after they've been picked. Let them ripen for a few days at room temperature, until the flesh is just barely soft around the neck near the stem. They won't necessarily change color when ripe. Bartlett pears can be stored unripe but not quite as long as the winter pears; they'll turn from green to golden when ripe.

POMEGRANATES

The pomegranate is native to Persia and is one of the most historically meaningful fruits, featuring prominently in myths and legends—from its supposed beginnings in the blood of Adonis, to its role in the ancient Greek story of Persephone, who ate pomegranate seeds in the Underworld and was thus condemned to stay there for half the year (hence fall and winter), to the Hebrew Bible's Song of Solomon and its status as one of the Seven Species of Israel.

You probably won't find pomegranates in your local farmers' market, but they'll be available all fall and into winter in most good supermarkets. Also look for them in Asian grocery stores, where they might be less expensive (if a bit smaller). The most important indicator of a good pomegranate is weight: the heavier, the better for juicy seeds. The skin's color may be bright pink to dark red to tannish brown; there are white and black pomegranates, but they are rare outside the Middle East. Some varieties of pomegranate yield typical garnet-colored seeds; some have pale pink or white seeds.

The best way to separate the seeds (technically the arils) from the skin and white pith and membrane that surround them is to use a sharp paring knife to cut a small cone-shaped piece from the top to reveal the lines of pith that separate the sections filled with arils. Score the outside of the skin from top to bottom along the lines of pith, keeping the cut shallow, so you cut into as few of the arils as possible, then submerge the pomegranate in a bowl of cold water and use your hands to pull it apart into sections. (Doing this under water will keep the deep-red juice from splattering and staining countertops and clothes.) Continue to separate the membrane from the arils, letting the arils sink to the bottom of the bowl and the membrane and pith float to the surface of the water to be scooped out and discarded. Drain the seeds in a colander.

Whole pomegranates can be kept in a loosely closed plastic bag or container in the refrigerator for up to a month. The separated, drained seeds can be refrigerated for up to a week or frozen for several months.

PARSNIPS

Closely related to and as sweet as or sweeter than carrots, these snowy white winter root vegetables should be used in desserts much more than they are. Try them in place of carrots or even sweet potatoes or pumpkin in cakes and pies. You can also simply caramelize them in a sauté pan with butter and a pinch of sweet spices, maybe with a squeeze of citrus and drizzle of honey.

Parsnips are a cold-weather farmers' market staple and are at their sweetest after they've experienced a hard frost or two in the ground: The cold encourages them to convert their starches to sugar, so keep an eye on the almanac. Look for roots that are heavy and stiff, not bendable, preferably with fresh-looking greens still attached.

Take the time to peel parsnips (mostly to get rid of the hairy side roots), then quarter them lengthwise and use the peeler or a sharp knife to scrape out the center core, which can be not only woody and tough but bitter.

Parsnips will keep for several weeks in a plastic bag in the crisper drawer of the refrigerator—just like carrots.

PANTRY STAPLES, SUPPLIES & TECHNIQUES

THESE DESSERTS ARE, FOR THE MOST PART, SIMPLE AFFAIRS. You don't need much in the way of equipment to produce an excellent dessert made with the best basic ingredients and in-season produce: an uncomplicated filling; a frosting or quick glaze; perhaps an informal sprinkle of coarse sugar or garnish of fresh fruit or herbs. I'm a big fan of using the right tools for the job and the best versions of those tools available to me within reason, but I don't like unnecessary clutter in my kitchen, and I don't like spending more money than I have to. What follows are my recommendations for the bare essentials you'll need to make the recipes in this book. You probably have most of them already.

These desserts also won't require you to master a lot of difficult skills—simply follow the recipes and refer to the descriptions of basic techniques in this chapter if you're not familiar with how to cream butter and sugar, for example, or what it means to whip egg whites until stiff peaks form. Your desserts will be lovely, delicious, and, most important, homemade.

PANTRY STAPLES

The basic building blocks of most of my cakes are fat (butter or oil), sugar, eggs, flour, milk, and salt. While some deviation from my preferred ingredients is probably inevitable—and in fact I encourage you to experiment!—to ensure the best results, it makes sense to use ingredients that are as close to the ones I use as possible. If a recipe calls for all-purpose flour and you use whole-wheat, the outcome might not be as you'd expect. Likewise if your butter is salted instead of unsalted, or at a different starting temperature.

BUTTER & OILS

I use unsalted butter. It doesn't keep as well as salted (if you have large quantities, freeze it), but it's easier to control the amount of salt in baked goods when you're starting from a clean slate. If a recipe says that the butter should be "chilled," it means straight from the fridge. If a recipe says the butter should be "at room temperature" or "softened," let it sit out on the counter for at least two hours beforehand (if you're able to plan ahead, pull the butter out the night before you bake). You might be tempted to speed up softening by popping the stick in a microwave, but be careful: Use short bursts of ten seconds at a time, or you're likely to end up with partially to fully melted butter, which won't behave in the same way as solid butter. If it accidentally melts, start over with new butter. (And pop some popcorn for the melted stuff.)

I also occasionally use vegetable oil—any light-colored flavorless vegetable oil, like canola,

safflower, or grapeseed, will work. Cakes made with oil tend to be finer-textured than cakes made with butter; of course then they lack butter flavor, but sometimes that isn't as important as texture. Olive oil can be wonderful in cakes. It adds a fruity, slightly savory flavor and aroma and results in a cake of exceptional tenderness and fine texture because it contains emulsifiers that regular vegetable oil lacks. You can use good-quality extra-virgin if you'd like the flavor to shine through, or a milder virgin or "light" olive oil (or even a combination of olive and neutral vegetable oils) for more subtlety.

SUGAR & OTHER SWEETENERS

I prefer sugar that's specifically labeled "cane sugar"; otherwise, it's likely to be beet sugar. If you don't have a preference, either will work fine here.

Dark and light brown sugars are simply refined white granulated sugar to which more or less molasses has been added; I use them when I want that dark butterscotch flavor in a cake, or when I want a moister crumb. If you only have dark or light, in a pinch you can use them interchangeably.

Molasses is a dark syrup that's a by-product of sugar production. Use an all-purpose dark molasses rather than a mild-flavored light molasses or blackstrap molasses, which is darker, spicier, and less sweet.

Honey, as you might expect, plays a huge

role in my baking. Aside from the lovely floral notes honey adds to baked goods, honey has a positive effect on a cake's keeping qualities. Because honey is hygroscopic, which means it absorbs water, a honey-sweetened cake will draw moisture from the air and stay moist longer. Any wildflower or clover honey will work well, but try experimenting with local honeys—orange blossom, sage, and buckwheat all have interesting flavors. Your farmers' market should have a decent selection to choose from.

EGGS

Use fresh local eggs from hens who are allowed to roam with relative freedom, eating whatever seeds or unfortunate insects cross their path, and your baked goods will benefit greatly. At the very least, use good eggs when making a cake in which the eggs—or the color of the yolks—will be most noticeable. My recipes are based on standard large eggs; use your judgment if your farm-fresh eggs are a little smaller or larger. In most cases, eggs should be at room temperature before you start mixing. You can leave the whole eggs on the counter for a couple hours, or speed up the process by submerging them in warm water for fifteen to twenty minutes before cracking them.

FLOUR

Here in the South, bakers like soft white winter wheat (White Lily brand is the most famous example), which yields tender cakes and the fluffiest biscuits you've ever seen. If you can find White Lily, use that when the recipe calls for all-purpose flour. If White Lily isn't available, your next best bet is to look for a specialty all-purpose flour that is labeled "soft white winter wheat";

otherwise, any all-purpose flour will do.

For especially fine-crumbed cakes, I like to use cake flour, which is made from soft wheat, much lower in protein than all-purpose flour, and more finely milled, so it's fluffier. Most cake flour (King Arthur's being a prominent exception) has been bleached; this has the effect not only of making the flour super–bright white but also of making it slightly more acidic, so it reacts differently with chemical leaveners like baking powder. White Lily or a similar Southern-style flour is a good stand-in for cake flour; you can also replace 2 tablespoons out of each cup (130 g) of regular all-purpose flour called for with 2 tablespoons cornstarch.

I also use whole-wheat flour in some of my cakes, not only because it's relatively healthful but because it imparts a subtly sweet nutty flavor. If you don't go through your flour supply fairly quickly, consider storing whole-wheat flour in the freezer, as the oils in the wheat bran can go rancid after a time at room temperature.

I call for self-rising flour in one recipe (page 56); this is simply all-purpose flour to which leavener and a bit of salt have been added. If you don't have self-rising flour, you can make your own: Put 1½ teaspoons baking powder and ¼ teaspoon salt in a measuring cup and spoon in enough all-purpose flour to make 1 cup (130 g).

Cornmeal is another staple in my pantry. For cakes, I use fine-ground yellow cornmeal. Stone-ground or a coarser grind (like cornmeal grits or polenta) tend to yield a grainy crumb and are best left for homey cornbread—or the polenta cake recipe on page 215.

Almond and hazelnut flour or meal are available in good grocery stores and in natural foods stores. You can make your own in a pinch by grinding whole or blanched almonds or hazelnuts in a food processor or blender with a pinch or two of sugar to keep the meal from clumping. That said, if the nut flour is a major component of a cake, it's best to use store-bought, which is finer and more powdery than homemade. Nut flours will last longer if they're kept in sealed containers in the freezer to prevent the nut oils from going rancid.

MILK

For best results, use whole milk in these recipes. It contains 3.5 to 4 percent fat, and because fat is a tenderizer and moisturizer, the texture of your cake will benefit. If you don't generally keep whole milk on hand, you can use lower-fat or skim milk and replace a bit of it with half-and-half (10 to 15 percent fat) or heavy cream (36 to 40 percent fat).

I also use buttermilk in some of my cakes; its acid reacts with the leaveners to make fluffy cakes and also helps to inhibit gluten formation in flour. Any cultured buttermilk, with its distinctive tang and thickness, will work fine.

SALT

I use table salt (iodized salt) in the recipes here because it's finer and easier to measure accurately than coarse kosher salt and because it distributes throughout batters and doughs more evenly.

SUPPLIES

MEASURING CUPS & SPOONS

Whatever measuring cups and spoons you have already will work just fine, of course, but if you're just beginning to outfit your kitchen for baking, look for nesting stainless-steel dry measuring cups: a set that includes a 1-cup, ½-cup, ⅓-cup, and ¼-cup measure should do it; ¾-cup, ⅔-cup, and ⅛-cup (2-tablespoon) ones are great to have but not necessary. If you do a lot of baking, consider getting two sets so you don't have to wash and dry them midrecipe. Metal cups with sturdy handles (the better to scoop with and pack stiff brown sugar into, for example) will last longer than plastic and can be slightly more accurate as you scrape a straight edge across the top. You'll also need a glass liquid measuring cup (with markings on two sides for accuracy): a 2-cup (480-ml) or 4-cup (960-ml) one—or, better, both—will work.

I prefer stainless-steel measuring spoons over plastic or ceramic, and I like the ones with deeper rather than shallower bowls: They're more accurate because there's less surface area to scrape off evenly. You'll need a set with 1-tablespoon, 1-teaspoon, ½-teaspoon, ¼-teaspoon, and ⅛-teaspoon spoons; a ¾-teaspoon one is useful but not absolutely necessary.

ELECTRIC MIXER

I used a KitchenAid five-quart stand mixer with a paddle attachment, whisk attachment, and dough hook to test all of these recipes, so your results will be closer to mine if you have something similar. For most recipes, you can get away with using a handheld electric mixer with beaters, but there are a few that involve adding an ingredient to the bowl gradually while the mixer is running, and this is much easier if you have two hands free (or a friend in the kitchen). Making a boiled frosting, for example, or a buttercream that starts with a cooked meringue, requires you to whip egg whites and then slowly pour a hot syrup into the whites as they whip—I wouldn't recommend doing this without a stand mixer.

FOOD PROCESSOR

A food processor may take up counter or storage space, but it's invaluable in my kitchen. I use it to grind almonds and hazelnuts, to puree fruits for easily spreadable jams and cake fillings, to quickly shred zucchini and carrots for cakes using the grating blade, and a host of other tasks that don't have anything to do with cake baking. If you can't justify the expense or the space, consider using a mini food processor and working in batches, when necessary, supplementing it with a good sturdy flat or box grater.

MIXING BOWLS

Have a good number of bowls of all sizes on hand. For my main mixing bowls, I like—again—stainless steel, because it's nonreactive (that is, it won't react with acidic ingredients like lemon juice or fruit), easy to clean thoroughly (unlike

plastic, which can retain traces of oil and other fats even after vigorous scrubbing, hampering your egg-white-whipping efforts), and heatproof (which means they can be set atop a saucepan of simmering water to make a double boiler, and you can pour hot ingredients into them with no adverse effects). Have one or two large bowls, two or three medium bowls, and several smaller bowls big enough for, say, mixing cinnamon and sugar for sprinkling, or a crumb topping.

UTENSILS

You might not need all of these tools for every recipe here, but for the most part, these are all fairly basic items. They'll take you far, whether you're baking from this book or any other one.

Have at least a couple flexible rubber spatulas, not too large, for mixing and for scraping out bowls. A heatproof silicone spatula is useful for stirring mixtures on the stovetop—fruit jams and compotes, sugar syrups, melted butter or chocolate, and so on.

Not just for stirring and mixing, a wooden spoon is what you need for cooking a custard and determining when it's thick enough to coat the back of the spoon.

These are seasonal desserts, which means there's a lot of fruit and vegetables here, and much of that produce will need to be peeled, chopped, cored, diced, or sliced. Any cutting board will do; just make sure it's heavy and not warped, and put a damp kitchen towel underneath to stabilize it, if necessary. A good fruit and vegetable peeler will come in handy—I like the Y-shaped ones, but use whatever kind feels comfortable in your hand. For peeling soft fruits like mangoes, peaches, and tomatoes, a serrated vegetable peeler is a godsend, though of course you can also just blanch peaches and

> ### STOCKING SMALL BOWLS
>
> I'd like to make a case for having a good number of very small bowls on hand. Small bowls are great for setting up a *mise-en-place*, holding measured ingredients like spices or sugar or fresh-squeezed lemon juice so they're ready when you need them and you won't have to scramble to find measuring cups or spoons and scoop out quantities in a hurry.
>
> They're also useful for cracking eggs into one at a time before transferring the egg to your main bowl. That way you can pick out any bits of shell before they disappear into the batter, and the whole batch won't be compromised if an egg happens to be rotten.

tomatoes in boiling water for a few seconds and slip off the peels.

A supersharp Microplane-type grater is a brilliant tool for finely grating zest and nutmeg (which should always be freshly grated). Try using it to grate a cinnamon stick for an intensely flavorful garnish.

An old-fashioned sifter, with a handle and bail that scrapes dry ingredients through a sieve is quick and easy to use, but a regular medium-size fine-mesh wire sieve works just as well and isn't quite as single-use as a sifter. A small sieve is handy for sifting powdered sugar over cakes and for straining seeds and pulp from lemon juice.

For smoothing the tops of cake batter in the pan, dolloping and spreading icing, or adding decorative swoops to meringues and frostings, nothing beats an offset, or angled, stainless-steel spatula. A good size to start with is one that has a blade about 1¼ inches (30 mm) wide and about 7 inches (17 cm) long. A smaller spatula will be useful for frosting cupcakes and for detail work.

A bench scraper (also called a bench knife) is a handy tool—it's basically a wide rectangular spatula with a sharp edge made for scraping pastry and bread doughs from the work surface, but you'll find lots of uses for it. Use it to scrape a clean, smooth surface onto frosted layer cakes or to scoop chopped fruits and vegetables from a cutting board into a bowl or pan. Bench scrapers with wood handles can get a little grimy over time; all-stainless-steel ones are a better choice.

If you plan to get fancy, invest in a box of disposable plastic or reusable canvas or heavy-duty plastic piping bags. You'll also need a two-part plastic adaptor (the adaptor base that goes inside the bag as well as the ring that screws onto it to secure the metal tip to the bag). These come in two sizes, so make sure you have the size that fits your tips. You can buy a set of decorator tips or purchase them individually. For the most basic piping purposes, try a medium or large plain round tip, plus one or two open or closed star tips. I've also been known to use a zip-tight plastic bag in a pinch—just snip off the corner, push your tip snugly in, and fill the bag with frosting.

OVEN & CANDY THERMOMETERS

Your oven almost certainly already has a built-in thermometer, but it's also almost certainly inaccurate. This is fine if you're roasting vegetables, but not if you're making cakes, which are much more susceptible to variations in baking conditions. You can get a decent-enough oven thermometer at just about any supermarket, and it'll be worth the investment. At the very least, it will indicate when your oven has fully preheated; yours may beep when it thinks it has come up to temperature, but check the actual thermometer and you might be surprised to see that it's not even close.

You'll also need a candy thermometer, which is essential for making meringue-style frostings. Any kind will do, but I prefer a probe thermometer with a digital readout for accuracy. Before you use it for the first time, you should calibrate it, or at least note how far off its readings are: Put the probe in fully boiling water, and it should read 212°F (100°C) if you're at sea level (or a bit less if you live at a higher altitude—water boils at lower temperatures as the elevation increases). If it's off by a few degrees from what you expect, jot down the difference and keep that in mind as you use the thermometer in the future.

COOLING RACKS

You should have two or three wire racks for cooling cake layers. If counter space is limited, looks for racks that unfold and can be stacked atop one another.

TECHNIQUES

MEASURING INGREDIENTS

Probably the most important aspect of baking is accurate measuring. If you do this part right, you're at least halfway down the road to a great cake. The first thing to know is that solids and liquids are usually measured differently. To measure solids, use graduated individual measuring cups; to measure liquids, use a large glass measuring cup with markings on the side. Measuring with a scale is helpful, but not essential for my recipes. For those folks who already own a scale, I've included the metric equivalents.

Flour: Put a sheet of waxed paper (or any kind of paper) on the counter and put your measuring cup in the center of it. Use a large spoon to stir the flour in the bag or storage container so it's evenly aerated, then spoon it into the cup until the level rises well above the rim. Use a straight edge (like a knife, spoon handle, or clean ruler) to scrape the excess off the top, leveling the flour with the rim of the measuring cup. Don't tap the flour down or pack it into the cup, or you might end up with too much flour in your recipe. Dump the cup of flour into your mixing bowl and repeat, using different cup measures as needed, until you have the quantity you need. When you're done measuring, lift the paper and dump the excess flour back into the bag.

When measuring cornmeal and nut flours, use the method above but be especially careful to stir out any lumps.

Sugar and other sweeteners: Granulated (white) sugar can be simply scooped from the bag or container with a measuring cup—be sure to break up any lumps. Brown sugar should be firmly packed into the cup and leveled off with a straight edge. Brown sugar has a tendency to form small, hard lumps in storage; if yours is very lumpy, push it through a sieve before measuring.

Molasses and honey can be measured in graduated cups or a glass measure. To make extraction of the sticky stuff a breeze, lightly spray the inside of the measuring cup with nonstick cooking spray or vegetable oil before you pour it in—it'll slide right out.

Leaveners and salt: Make sure there are no lumps in your baking powder and baking soda, then fill a measuring spoon and level the surface. Don't be tempted to just use one measuring spoon and eyeball half teaspoons and such: For 1½ teaspoons, use a 1-teaspoon and a ½-teaspoon measure for accuracy.

Butter: For butter, use the markings on the wrapping as a guide.

Liquids: Use a glass measuring cup with cup markings and a spout for dripless, mess-free pouring. Be sure it's on a level surface and that the liquid aligns with the markings on either side of the cup.

CREAMING BUTTER & SUGAR

Many cake recipes ask you to whisk together the dry ingredients (flour, leavening, any spices, salt) in one bowl and beat or "cream" the butter and sugar in another bowl. What is creaming and why do we do it? Creaming simply means vigorously beating room-temperature or softened butter together with sugar until the mixture is light and fluffy. The violent action forces the individual granules of sugar throughout the butter, which opens up air pockets that will expand when the batter is baked, resulting in a light and fluffy cake.

First cut the butter into pieces and beat it on its own until it's smooth and soft. (Use an electric mixer fitted with the paddle attachment for best results; otherwise, you'll end up with either a very tired spatula-wielding arm or an underbeaten mixture.) Then add the sugar and continue to beat, stopping and scraping down the sides of the bowl occasionally, until the mixture is lighter in color and very fluffy. This could take 3 minutes or longer. Don't skimp on this step, as it's essential to a light cake.

WHIPPING
CREAM & EGG WHITES

To whip cream: Chill a metal mixing bowl in the refrigerator or freezer, along with a whisk or the whisk attachment of an electric mixer, until very cold. Start with well-chilled heavy cream (also labeled "whipping cream"; it should be at least 36 percent fat in order to thicken properly). Pour it into the chilled bowl and use the chilled whisk to beat it until it starts to thicken. Sprinkle in the sugar—either powdered or granulated—and continue to whisk until soft peaks form when you lift the whisk from the cream.

To whip egg whites: Beating egg whites is a technique used not only in sponge cake and angel food cake batters but also in frostings. Make sure your electric mixer's metal bowl and whisk attachment are perfectly clean and dry: No trace of oil or other fat should come into contact with the egg whites, or they won't inflate fully. Also make sure your hands and anything the egg whites will touch as they're being separated from the yolks are clean and dry. Bring the egg whites

to room temperature, either by warming the whole eggs in their shells in a bowl of warm water for ten minutes before separating the whites and yolks or by putting the whites in a bowl and setting the bowl in a shallow pan of warm water.

Put the whites in the clean mixer bowl and whisk on low speed until they are foamy, then increase the speed to medium and whisk until they can hold their shape (at which point you can begin gradually adding sugar, if the recipe calls for it), then increase the speed to high and beat just until they hold stiff peaks that don't droop when the whisk is lifted. Don't overbeat (it's important not to walk away from the mixer while the motor is running) or the whites will dry out and take on a curdled appearance; if that happens, start over.

FOLDING
INGREDIENTS TOGETHER

Often a recipe will ask you to fold an airy mixture (like whipped egg whites) into a denser mixture (like whole eggs or egg yolks and sugar); the idea is to combine the two without deflating the airy mixture. Using a rubber spatula, stir a scoopful of the light mixture into the dense mixture until it's just incorporated. Then gently scoop about a third of the remaining light mixture onto the dense; using the spatula, cut down through the center of the mixture to the bottom of the bowl, scrape the bottom of the bowl to the edge, and gently lift the denser mixture from the bottom up and over the top of the light mixture. Rotate the bowl. Repeat until the mixture—the cake batter or the cream— is evenly colored and both ingredients are incorporated, with no streaks remaining. Don't stir in a circular motion, but instead cut and lift, to keep the mixture from deflating.

Use the same folding technique—cutting, lifting, and turning—when folding dry ingredients (like sifted flour and leavener) into a light and airy substance (like whipped egg whites). Sift about a quarter of the dry ingredients at a time over the light mixture and fold gently to incorporate each addition.

When the two mixtures being folded together are a light, airy one (like whipped cream) and a liquid but not stiff mixture (like melted chocolate), usually the liquid mixture is drizzled onto the light mixture and folded in as above.

PREPARING CAKE PANS

I almost always prepare my cake pans in some way before pouring or spreading in batter. Often I just give the bottom and sides—and any corners or Bundt-pan nooks and crannies—a light coating of soft butter (if you have a paper wrapper from a stick of butter, use that to spread it). Sometimes a heavier coating is needed.

If the cake is especially prone to sticking to the pan, I'll butter the pan, then line the bottom with parchment paper, then butter the paper as well. To cut a round of parchment the size you need, you have a couple of options: You can use the bottom of the pan as a template, trace a circle onto the paper, and cut it out. Or you can cut a square of paper larger than the pan, fold it in half, then quarters, then fold the quartered paper into a triangle and then another narrower triangle (always matching the folded edges). Hold the point of the triangle (the center of the square of paper) over the center of the pan and cut off the opposite side of the triangle where it meets the edge of the pan. Unfold and you should have a rough circle of paper the size of your pan bottom.

Occasionally, I'll ask you to butter and flour a cake pan. To do this, butter the pan, line it

CAKE PANS

Here are the pans I use in these recipes:

- 6-, 8-, 9-, and 10-inch (15-, 20-, 23-, and 25-cm) round cake pans (you might need more than one of each; check the recipe before you start mixing)

- 9-inch (23-cm) springform pan

- 8-inch (20-cm) square pan

- 9-by-13-inch (23-by-33-cm) baking pan

- 10-inch (25-cm) tube pan, with removable bottom

- 10-inch (25-cm) Bundt pan

- 10-by-15-inch (25-by-38-cm) jelly-roll pan

- 9-inch (23-cm) cast-iron skillet

- 9-inch (23-cm) pie plate

- Standard 12-cup (3½-ounce/100 g) muffin pan

- Large 6-cup (7-ounce/200 g) muffin pan

- 9-by-5-inch (23-by-12-cm) loaf pan

I prefer light-colored, professional-style metal pans—not nonstick—with straight (rather than angled) sides. For the 9-by-13-inch (23-by-33-cm) pan, either metal or glass is fine.

with parchment, if necessary, then sprinkle in a tablespoon or so of flour. Tap and tilt the pan so that the flour coats the bottom and sides of the pan, sticking to the butter. Dump out and discard any excess flour. For chocolate cakes that are to be served with the outer surfaces showing, dust with cocoa powder instead of flour, which can leave white spots if it adheres to the butter too enthusiastically or unevenly.

For cupcakes, simply put paper liners in the cups.

CHECKING CAKES FOR DONENESS

Every cake is different, and in each recipe, I give you details about how to tell when the cake is done. The most common way to test for doneness is to insert a special cake tester utensil or a toothpick or bamboo skewer into the center of the cake and pull it out; depending on the recipe, doneness might be indicated by the presence of a few wet crumbs, dry crumbs, or no crumbs clinging to the tester.

USING A PIPING BAG

I'm convinced that most people would not use piping bags at all if there weren't a trick to filling them without fuss. Luckily, there are two easy ways to get icing from bowl to bag. But before you get started with that, you need to attach the tip: Remove the ring from the plastic coupler base. Using a disposable plastic pastry bag or a zip-tight plastic freezer bag, insert the coupler base into the closed corner of the bag and push it down tightly. Make a mark with your thumbnail about ¼ inch (6 mm) below the lowest screw thread—the ridge you can see through the bag. Scoot the coupler base out of the way and cut the

corner of the bag off at the line you marked, then push the coupler back into place. Put the tip on the coupler and then screw the ring on over the tip to hold it securely.

Now hold the bag loosely with your non-dominant hand and fold the open end back over your fist to form a wide cuff that covers your hand. With a spatula in the other hand, scoop frosting into the bag and squeeze the thumb and forefinger of the hand holding the bag to wipe the spatula clean. You can also put the bag, tip down, in a glass measuring cup or large jar and fold the top down over the rim of the jar to keep it free of icing while you fill it; this technique has the advantage of leaving both hands free, since the measuring cup or jar will hold the bag upright while you fill it.

Unfold the "cuff" of the bag and seal the open end by twisting it or rolling it tightly toward the tip. Grip the twisted or rolled part of the bag with one hand and put the other hand just below it, toward the tip. Squeeze the frosting down toward the tip, applying most of the pressure with the hand on the twisted or rolled-up part of the bag. Before aiming it at your cake, pipe a bit of icing back out into the bowl to push the air out of the tip.

FROSTING CAKES

Most of my cakes are, shall we say, rustic-looking. I'm much more concerned with flavor, texture, and overall deliciousness than aesthetics. My frosting is rarely perfectly smooth and even, and my cake decorating usually takes the form of fresh seasonal fruit or a swoop of whipped cream—again, it's all about flavor for me. That

said, there's something very special about a stunningly beautiful layer cake perched atop a vintage milk glass pedestal illuminated by an array of slender birthday candles or jeweled with candied rose petals or simply, artfully dolloped with a glossy meringue frosting. Particularly on special occasions, I do try to make my cakes look as luscious as they taste.

When frosting round layer cakes, a cake-decorating turntable or lazy Susan will make the cake-frosting periods of your life easier (if you're not using a turntable, just use a cake serving platter). Put a little dab of frosting in the center to hold the bottom cake layer steady, then set the first layer on it, with the most even, smooth side up. Scoop some frosting or filling onto the center of the layer and use an offset spatula to spread it to the edges, slowly spinning the turntable if it helps you spread more evenly. It doesn't have to be perfectly smooth by any means. Put the second layer on top with the most even side up, and repeat until you get to the last layer, which should have the cake layer's bottom, flat and smooth, on top.

At this point you can simply frost the top and call it a day, or continue on and frost the sides as well. Dollop lots of frosting in the center of the top layer and use the spatula to spread it out and just over the edge. Try not to touch the cake itself with the spatula at all; it should come in contact only with frosting so that it doesn't pick up crumbs and spread them throughout the frosting. Next, scoop frosting onto the sides and spread it to roughly cover the sides.

You can also use a piping bag to evenly fill and frost cakes. Fit it with a medium plain or wide flat tip, fill the bag (see page 51), and pipe concentric circles, or rows if your cake is square or rectangular, over the surface. Pipe up and down the sides as well if you're frosting them, and smooth them according to your preferred method.

FROSTING TECHNIQUES

A piping bag can make frosting cupcakes a breeze, and there are dozens of ways you can put frosting to cake. This is a good excuse to jump on the Internet to find tutorials and pictures for inspiration. Following are a few of the easiest techniques I've come across.

ROSETTE: Use a medium star tip and pipe frosting onto the top in a tight spiral starting in the center and circling to the outer edge. If you'd like, when you've covered the entire surface, keep going to make one more swoop back to the center, lifting the piping-bag tip to make a peak.

SWIRL: Use a large star or plain tip and pipe frosting in a tight spiral starting at the outer edge of the cupcake and ending in the center;

release pressure on the piping bag and then lift it from the cupcake to make a peak.

PLAIN: You can also just use an offset spatula. Put a generous dollop of frosting on top, mounding it slightly in the center, and quickly spread it to the edges. Alternatively, use a cookie-dough or ice-cream scoop to plop evenly sized mounds of frosting onto the center of each cupcake.

Cupcakes are a great way to practice your piping skills: If you mess up, you can easily scrape off the offending frosting and start again. Try using a small star tip and covering the whole top with miniature rosettes. Or make fancy roses with a special wide rose-petal piping tip.

There are several ways to smooth the sides and top of a frosted cake. Use whichever one you feel most comfortable with, and recognize that it takes practice. Smooth the sides using either the offset spatula or a bench scraper held vertically and at a slight angle, removing excess frosting as you spin the turntable. This will create a small ridge of frosting at the top. Remove this with the spatula, then use the spatula to smooth the top.

You can also use the hot-spatula method: Dip the offset spatula in very hot water and dry it with a towel before each swipe as you level the frosting on top and sides with brief, quick motions. The heat will melt the frosting a bit and

create a slightly glossy finish.

Buttercream frosting can be smoothed with a good-quality, heavy-duty paper towel: Gently press the paper towel over the top of the frosting, smoothing it so it's flat and even, then peel it off and do the same thing to the sides. Smooth any texture left by the towel with a spatula.

Boiled frostings—those that are made like a meringue, with hot sugar syrup poured into whipping egg whites—are easy: Just spread the frosting over the whole cake in a reasonably even layer, then use the tip of the offset spatula to create swirls, lifting the frosting into pretty peaks all over the cake.

SPRING

Strawberry-Rhubarb
VICTORIA SPONGE
SERVES 8

When the days of winter seem unending, strawberries and rhubarb
are the light at the end of the tunnel. They practically sing the
sweetness of spring. While I love a classic strawberry rhubarb pie,
this is a mighty fine way to enjoy that combination too.

For the strawberry-rhubarb filling:

- 1 pound (455 g) rhubarb, stems only, cut into ½-inch (12-mm) pieces
- 2 cups (400 g) fresh strawberries, hulled and halved
- ¼ cup (50 g) granulated sugar
- ½ teaspoon vanilla extract

For the cake:

- 1 cup (2 sticks/225 g) unsalted butter, room temperature
- 1½ cups (300 g) granulated sugar
- 4 large eggs
- 1 teaspoon vanilla extract
- 3 cups (375 g) self-rising flour

For the whipped cream filling and assembly:

- 1½ cups (360 ml) heavy cream
- ¼ cup (25 g) powdered sugar, plus more for dusting
- ½ teaspoon vanilla extract

To make the strawberry-rhubarb filling: In a medium saucepan, combine the rhubarb, 1 cup (200 g) of the strawberries, and the sugar. Bring the mixture to a boil over medium-high heat. Reduce the heat to medium-low and cook until the rhubarb is tender, 5 to 7 minutes. Remove the pan from the heat and stir in the remaining 1 cup (200 g) strawberries and the vanilla. Set aside to cool completely.

To make the cake: Preheat the oven to 350°F (175°C). Butter two 8-inch (20-cm) round cake pans.

In the bowl of an electric mixer fitted with the paddle attachment, cream together the butter and sugar until light and fluffy, 3 to 5 minutes. Add the eggs one at a time, scraping down the sides of the bowl after each addition. Stir in the vanilla. Add the flour, beating until just combined.

Divide the mixture evenly between the prepared cake pans. The batter will be thick, so use a spatula to spread it.

Bake until a toothpick inserted in the center comes out clean, 20 to 25 minutes. Allow the layers to cool for 10 minutes in the pans before turning them out onto a wire rack to cool completely.

To make the whipped cream: In a chilled bowl, combine the cream, powdered sugar, and vanilla. Using a chilled whisk, whip by hand or with an electric mixer until soft peaks form.

To assemble the cake: Place one cake layer on a serving plate, spread the strawberry-rhubarb filling on top, and cover with the whipped cream. Set the second layer on top and dust the cake with powdered sugar just before serving.

STRAWBERRY LAYER CAKE

with Strawberry-Basil Buttercream

SERVES 8

With its bright pink frosting and fluffy layers,
this is a celebration cake through and through.

To make the strawberry puree: In a small saucepan, combine
the strawberries and sugar and simmer over medium-low heat for
15 minutes, or until soft. Allow the mixture to cool, then pour it
into a blender and puree until smooth.

To make the cake: Preheat the oven to 350°F (175°C). Butter
three 8-inch (20-cm) round cake pans and line the bottoms with
buttered parchment.

In a medium bowl, whisk together the flour, baking powder,
and salt.

In the bowl of an electric mixer fitted with the paddle
attachment, cream together the butter and sugar until light and
fluffy, 3 to 5 minutes. Add the eggs one at a time, scraping down
the sides of the bowl after each addition.

In a measuring cup, combine the milk and strawberry puree.

Alternate adding the flour mixture and the strawberry milk to
the mixer bowl, beginning and ending with the flour.

Divide the batter evenly among the prepared pans, smoothing
the tops. Bake for 25 to 30 minutes, until a toothpick inserted into
the center of the cakes comes out clean. Transfer the pans to wire
racks for 10 minutes, then unmold and peel off the parchment paper.

To make the frosting: In the bowl of an electric mixer fitted with
the paddle attachment, beat the butter until pale and creamy,
3 to 5 minutes. Reduce the speed and add 1 cup (100 g) of the
powdered sugar. Add half the strawberry puree and the salt and
beat to combine. Add the remaining 2 to 3 cups (200 to 300 g)
powdered sugar and the remaining strawberry puree, and add
milk, as needed. Add the basil and stir.

To assemble the cake: Place one cake layer on a serving plate,
spread the frosting on top, then spread on a layer of strawberry
puree. Add the next cake layer and repeat. Add the top cake layer
and cover the outside of the cake with frosting.

For the strawberry puree:
**4 cups (800 g) fresh
strawberries,
hulled and halved**
¼ cup (50 g) granulated sugar

For the cake:
3 cups (420 g) cake flour
3½ teaspoons baking powder
1 teaspoon salt
**1 cup (2 sticks/225 g) unsalted
butter**
2 cups (400 g) granulated sugar
4 large eggs
¼ cup (60 ml) whole milk
**¾ cup (180 ml) strawberry
puree (see above)**

For the frosting:
**2 cups (4 sticks/450 g) unsalted
butter**
**3 to 4 cups (300 to 400 g)
powdered sugar**
**6 tablespoons (90 ml)
strawberry puree (see above)**
Pinch of salt
Whole milk, as needed
**1 tablespoon finely chopped
fresh basil**

Black Pepper-Roasted Strawberry
BUTTERMILK CAKE

SERVES 8

When strawberries are back in season, I always end up
buying baskets and baskets of them from my farmers' market.
Inevitably, there are a few that don't get eaten in time and are
almost overripe. Roasting them with black pepper intensifies
their flavor and creates puddles of jammy sweetness.

If you've got small strawberries, don't bother halving them.
You want sizable bites of strawberry throughout the cake.

For the roasted strawberries:

**1 pound (455 g) fresh
strawberries, hulled and
halved**

2 tablespoons olive oil

2 tablespoons granulated sugar

**¼ teaspoon freshly ground
black pepper**

For the cake:

**1½ cups (170 g) all-purpose
flour**

1 teaspoon baking powder

½ teaspoon salt

**½ cup (1 stick/115 g) unsalted
butter, room temperature**

1 cup (200 g) granulated sugar

2 large eggs

1 teaspoon vanilla extract

½ cup (120 ml) buttermilk

To roast the strawberries: Preheat the oven to 400°F (205°C).
Line a baking sheet with parchment paper.

In a medium bowl, combine the strawberries, oil, sugar, and
pepper. Arrange the berries in a single layer on the prepared
baking sheet. Roast them for 20 to 25 minutes, or until they are
soft. Allow them to cool.

To make the cake: Reduce the oven temperature to 350°F (175°C).
Butter a 9-inch (23-cm) round cake pan or 9-inch (23-cm) cast-
iron skillet.

In a medium bowl, whisk together the flour, baking powder,
and salt.

In the bowl of an electric mixer fitted with the paddle attachment, cream the butter and sugar until light and fluffy, 3 to 5
minutes. Add the eggs one at a time, beating well and scraping
down the sides of the bowl after each addition. Add the vanilla.

Alternately add the flour mixture and buttermilk to the mixer
bowl, beginning and ending with the flour.

Pour the batter into the prepared cake pan and top it with
the strawberries. Bake until a toothpick inserted in the center
comes out clean, 25 to 30 minutes. Allow the cake to cool for
10 minutes in the pan before turning out onto a wire rack to cool
completely.

Frozen
STRAWBERRY
CHEESECAKE

SERVES 8

I'm not usually one for decadent desserts—I prefer rustic, homey flavors—but this frozen cheesecake makes me a believer in indulgence. There's something so enticing about the contrast between the creamy cold cheesecake and the warm salted fudge sauce.

To make the crust: In a medium bowl, stir together the graham cracker crumbs and butter. Press them into the bottom of a 9-inch (23-cm) springform pan. Place the pan in the freezer while you make the filling.

To make the filling: In a small saucepan, combine half the strawberries, the granulated sugar, and 2 tablespoons water. Bring the mixture to a boil over medium-high heat, reduce the heat to medium-low, and allow to simmer until the berries are soft and the liquid is syrupy. Remove the pan from the heat and allow the berries to cool.

In the bowl of an electric mixer fitted with the paddle attachment, beat the cream cheese and yogurt. Add the powdered sugar and the strawberry mixture and mix until combined. Stir in the remaining strawberries. Pour the filling over the graham cracker crust and smooth the top. Freeze the cake until firm, about 4 hours or overnight.

To make the fudge sauce: In a medium saucepan, combine the cream, corn syrup, brown sugar, cocoa powder, and salt and bring to a simmer over medium heat. Add the chocolate, butter, and vanilla and stir until melted. Reduce the heat to low and allow the sauce to simmer, stirring occasionally, for 5 minutes, then remove it from the heat and allow it to cool to slightly.

Pour the fudge sauce over the top of the cheesecake.

For the crust:
- 1½ cups (130 g) graham cracker crumbs (from about 12 whole crackers)
- 3 tablespoons (45 g) unsalted butter, melted

For the filling:
- 1 pound (455 g) fresh strawberries, hulled and quartered
- ¼ cup (50 g) granulated sugar
- 2 (8-ounce/226-g) packages cream cheese, softened
- 1 cup (240 ml) vanilla Greek yogurt
- ¾ cup (75 g) powdered sugar

For the fudge sauce:
- ½ cup (120 ml) heavy cream
- ¼ cup (60 ml) light corn syrup
- ¼ cup (55 g) packed dark brown sugar
- ¼ cup (20 g) unsweetened cocoa powder
- ¼ teaspoon flaky sea salt
- 3 ounces (85 g) bittersweet chocolate, finely chopped
- 1½ tablespoons unsalted butter
- ½ teaspoon vanilla extract

STRAWBERRY-MINT SHORTCAKES

MAKES 6

Shortcake is maybe the most classic way of serving fresh strawberries, and for good reason. The warm, slightly sweet biscuit is the perfect vehicle for berries and whipped cream. I've stayed close to the original here (no need to fix what isn't broken!) and only added a bit of fresh mint to brighten the flavor.

For the strawberry-mint filling:

1 pound (455 g) fresh strawberries, hulled and quartered

2 tablespoons fresh mint leaves, roughly chopped

¼ cup (50 g) granulated sugar

For the shortcakes:

4 tablespoons (55 g) unsalted butter, chilled

1¾ cups (225 g) all-purpose flour

1 tablespoon baking powder

¼ teaspoon salt

1 tablespoon granulated sugar, plus more for sprinkling

¾ cup (180 ml) chilled heavy cream, plus more for brushing tops

For the whipped cream:

1 cup (240 ml) chilled heavy cream

2 tablespoons powdered sugar

To make the strawberry-mint filling: In a small bowl, combine the strawberries, mint, and sugar. Set them aside while you make the shortcakes, allowing the berries to macerate for at least 30 minutes.

To make the shortcakes: Preheat the oven to 375°F (190°C).

Grate the butter into a small bowl using the large side of a cheese grater. Stick the grated butter in the freezer for about 20 minutes.

In a large bowl, whisk together the flour, baking powder, salt, and sugar. Add the butter and cut it in with a fork. Add the cream and mix until just combined.

On a floured work surface, pat the dough into a round about ½ inch (12 mm) thick. Using a 3-inch (7.5-cm) biscuit cutter, cut out as many shortcakes as possible. Transfer them to a baking sheet, brush the tops with cream, and sprinkle them with sugar. Bake until the shortcakes are golden brown, 16 to 18 minutes. Transfer them to a wire rack and allow to cool slightly.

To make the whipped cream: Combine the cream and powdered sugar in a chilled bowl and, using a chilled whisk, whip by hand or with an electric mixer until soft peaks form.

To assemble the shortcakes: Cut the shortcakes in half horizontally and fill them with whipped cream and strawberry-mint filling. Be sure to pour some of the juice over the tops!

CHOCOLATE-CHERRY CUPCAKES

with Coffee Buttercream

MAKES 12

These cupcakes were inspired by a slice of Black Forest cake served with a demitasse of espresso I had once in a little café. I loved that pairing and just had to recreate it.

To make the cupcakes: Preheat the oven to 350°F (175°C). Line a cupcake pan with paper liners.

In a medium heatproof bowl, combine the butter and chocolate. Place the bowl over a simmering pot of water and stir until the mixture is melted and smooth. Allow to cool.

In a medium bowl, whisk together the flour, cocoa powder, baking powder, baking soda, and salt.

In a large bowl, whisk together the brown sugar, eggs, and vanilla. Stir in the cooled chocolate mixture. Alternate adding the flour mixture and buttermilk, beginning and ending with the flour. Stir in the cherries.

Divide the batter evenly among the paper liners, filling each two-thirds full. Bake for 17 to 20 minutes, until a toothpick inserted in the center comes out clean.

To make the buttercream: In the bowl of an electric mixer fitted with the whisk attachment, beat the egg yolks until they are pale in color, about 5 minutes.

In a small saucepan, bring the sugar and ¼ cup (60 ml) water to a rolling boil over medium-high heat. Pour this syrup into a glass measuring cup.

Drizzle a small amount of syrup into the yolks and beat for 5 seconds. Repeat this process until all the syrup is incorporated. Continue beating until the mixture has cooled.

Switch to the paddle attachment and add the butter one piece at a time until all has been incorporated. In a cup, dissolve the espresso powder in the hot water and beat it into the buttercream.

When the cupcakes have cooled, frost them and top them with the cherries.

For the cupcakes:
½ cup (1 stick/115 g) unsalted butter
4 ounces (115 g) bittersweet chocolate
1 cup (130 g) all-purpose flour
½ cup (40 g) unsweetened cocoa powder
1 teaspoon baking powder
½ teaspoon baking soda
¼ teaspoon salt
1 cup (220 g) packed light brown sugar
2 large eggs
1 teaspoon vanilla extract
½ cup (120 ml) buttermilk
1 cup (155 g) pitted, chopped fresh cherries

For the buttercream:
6 large egg yolks, room temperature
1 cup (200 g) granulated sugar
1 cup (2 sticks/225 g) unsalted butter, room temperature, cut into pieces
3 tablespoons instant espresso powder
1 tablespoon hot water

Whole cherries, for topping

Cherry-Almond
BROWN BUTTER CAKE

SERVES 8

I love this cake for its simplicity. It's easy to throw together before friends arrive—you don't need to pull out the mixer, and it only takes a few minutes total to prepare. If I'm feeling particularly decadent, I like to stir some dark chocolate chunks into the batter.

Melt the butter in a small saucepan over medium heat and cook, stirring occasionally, until it turns golden brown and nutty scented. Set aside.

Preheat the oven to 350°F (175°C). Butter a 9-inch (23-cm) round cake pan.

In a large bowl, whisk together the all-purpose flour, almond flour, sugar, baking powder, baking soda, and salt.

In a medium bowl, whisk together the milk, eggs, vanilla, almond extract, and the browned butter.

Pour the wet mixture into the dry mixture, stirring to combine. Stir in the cherries.

Pour the mixture into the prepared pan and sprinkle it with the almonds. Bake for 30 to 35 minutes, until the cake is golden brown and a toothpick inserted in the center comes out clean.

Allow to cool for 10 minutes in the pan before turning it onto a wire rack to cool completely. Dust the cake with powdered sugar before serving.

½ cup (1 stick/115 g) unsalted butter
1½ cups (170 g) all-purpose flour
½ cup (70 g) almond flour
1 cup (200 g) granulated sugar
2 teaspoons baking powder
½ teaspoon baking soda
¼ teaspoon salt
½ cup (120 ml) whole milk, room temperature
2 large eggs
1 teaspoon vanilla extract
½ teaspoon almond extract
½ cup (80 g) pitted whole fresh cherries
¼ cup (30 g) slivered almonds
Powdered sugar, for dusting

Dark Sweet Cherry
UPSIDE-DOWN CAKE

SERVES 8

My childhood was full of upside-down cakes, generally the classic pineapple-and-maraschino cherry type that's so often served at a church potluck. You can't go wrong with gooey caramelized fruit in a buttery cake batter, but my version adds depth to the sweet fruit with a bit of almond extract and balsamic vinegar.

¾ cup (1½ sticks/170 g) unsalted butter

¾ cup (165 g) packed light brown sugar

1 tablespoon balsamic vinegar

2 cups (310 g) pitted dark sweet cherries

1 cup (130 g) all-purpose flour

½ cup (70 g) almond flour

1 teaspoon baking powder

½ teaspoon baking soda

½ teaspoon salt

1 cup (200 g) granulated sugar

2 large eggs

1 teaspoon vanilla extract

½ teaspoon almond extract

½ cup (120 ml) whole milk

Preheat the oven to 350°F (175°C). Butter a 9-inch (23-cm) round cake pan.

Melt 4 tablespoons (½ stick/55 g) of the butter in a small saucepan over medium heat, then add the brown sugar and stir until dissolved. Stir in the vinegar. Pour the mixture into the prepared cake pan and place the cherries on top.

In a small bowl, whisk together the all-purpose flour, almond flour, baking powder, baking soda, and salt.

In the bowl of an electric mixer fitted with the paddle attachment, cream together the remaining ½ cup (1 stick/115 g) butter and the granulated sugar until light and fluffy, 3 to 4 minutes. Add the eggs one at a time, scraping down the sides of the bowl after each addition. Beat in the vanilla and the almond extract. Alternate adding the flour mixture and milk to the mixer bowl, beginning and ending with the flour.

Spread the batter over the cherries and bake until a toothpick inserted in the center comes out clean, about 30 minutes.

Let the cake cool in the pan for 15 minutes, then invert it onto a plate.

RHUBARB BUCKLE

with Custard Sauce

SERVES 8

Rhubarb and custard are a traditional British pairing, and one
I wholeheartedly support. The tart flavor of the rhubarb is
mellowed by the sweet creaminess of the custard sauce.

For the custard sauce:

3 large egg yolks
Pinch of salt
1 cup (240 ml) whole milk
⅓ cup (65 g) granulated sugar
½ teaspoon vanilla extract

For the crumble topping:

**½ cup (110 g) packed light
   brown sugar**
¾ cup (60 g) old-fashioned oats
¼ cup (30 g) all-purpose flour
½ teaspoon ground cinnamon
¼ teaspoon ground cardamom
Pinch of salt
**4 tablespoons (55 g) unsalted
   butter, melted**

For the cake:

2 cups (255 g) all-purpose flour
1 teaspoon baking powder
1 teaspoon ground ginger
½ teaspoon salt
**¾ cup (1 ½ sticks/170 g)
   unsalted butter**
1 cup (200 g) granulated sugar
1 large egg
½ cup (120 ml) buttermilk
**1 pound (455 g) rhubarb, stems
   only, cut into ½-inch (12-mm)
   pieces**

To make the custard sauce: Fill a large bowl with ice and cold
water, and set it nearby. In a medium bowl, whisk together the egg
yolks and salt.

   In a medium saucepan, bring the milk and sugar to a simmer
over medium heat. Slowly pour the hot milk mixture into the egg
yolks, whisking the entire time. Pour the milk and egg mixture
back into the saucepan and cook, stirring constantly, until the
mixture coats the back of a spoon.

   Remove the pan from the heat and stir in the vanilla. Pour
the sauce through a fine-mesh sieve into a heatproof bowl. Set the
bowl into the ice water. Let it cool to room temperature, stirring
occasionally. When the custard is cool, press plastic wrap directly
onto the surface and refrigerate it while making the cake.

To make the crumble topping: Combine the brown sugar, oats,
flour, cinnamon, cardamom, and salt in a medium bowl. Pour in
the butter and stir until clumps form. Place the bowl in the freezer
while you make the cake.

To make the cake: Preheat the oven to 350°F (175°C). Butter a
9-inch (23-cm) cast-iron skillet or round baking pan.

   In a medium bowl, whisk together the flour, baking powder,
ginger, and salt.

   In the bowl of an electric mixer fitted with the paddle
attachment, cream the butter and sugar until fluffy, 3 to 5
minutes. Beat in the egg. Add in half of the flour mixture, then the
buttermilk, then the rest of the flour. Gently mix in the rhubarb.
Pour the batter into the prepared pan. Top the cake with the
crumble topping.

   Bake for 35 to 40 minutes, until a toothpick inserted in the
center comes out clean. Allow it to cool completely. Serve it with a
generous helping of custard sauce.

HONEY CAKE

with Vanilla-Rhubarb Jam

SERVES 8

I wasn't a fan of rhubarb after having terrible rhubarb pie
as a teenager. But a few years ago, a friend offered me
some fresh from his garden. I couldn't turn him down, and
I decided to make a rhubarb jam, throwing in a vanilla
bean for good measure. Well, hello, deliciousness! It's great
slathered on a slice of this honey cake.

To make the jam: In a large pot, combine the rhubarb, sugar, lemon juice and zest, and vanilla bean seeds. Bring the mixture to a boil over medium-high heat, then reduce the heat to low and let the mixture simmer for 30 to 45 minutes, until it thickens and coats the back of a spoon.

Pour the jam into a clean jar. It will keep for up to 2 weeks.

To make the cake: Preheat the oven to 350°F (175°C). Butter a 9-by-5-inch (23-by-12-cm) loaf pan.

In a medium bowl, whisk together the flour, baking powder, baking soda, and salt.

In the bowl of an electric mixer fitted with the paddle attachment, cream together the butter and sugar until light and fluffy, 3 to 5 minutes. Beat in the eggs one at a time, scraping down the sides of the bowl after each addition. Add the honey and vanilla and beat for another minute.

Alternate adding the flour mixture and buttermilk to the mixer bowl, beginning and ending with the flour.

Pour the batter into the prepared pan, top it with raw sugar, and bake for 35 to 40 minutes, until a toothpick inserted in the center comes out clean.

Allow it to cool slightly, then cut the cake into slices and serve with a good dollop of vanilla-rhubarb jam.

For the jam:

1 pound (455 g) rhubarb, stems only, cut into 1-inch (2.5-cm) pieces
1 cup (200 g) granulated sugar
Juice and zest of 1 lemon
Seeds of 1 vanilla bean

For the cake:

2 cups (255 g) all-purpose flour
1 teaspoon baking powder
½ teaspoon baking soda
½ teaspoon salt
¾ cup (1½ sticks/170 g) unsalted butter
½ cup (100 g) granulated sugar
3 large eggs
½ cup (120 ml) wildflower honey
1 teaspoon vanilla extract
½ cup (120 ml) buttermilk
Raw sugar, for topping

Honeysuckle
BREEZE CAKE
SERVES 6 TO 8

I have so many memories of standing out in the woods
as a kid, sucking the sweet nectar out of the flowers. One
spring I tried to bottle that flavor and came up with this
honeysuckle syrup. When added to the frosting, it gives this
cake the sweet floral scent and taste of the blossoms.

For the honeysuckle water
and syrup:
**4 cups (100 g) honeysuckle
blossoms, lightly packed**
Boiling water
Granulated sugar

For the cake:
**1⅔ cups (215 g) all-purpose
flour**
2 teaspoons baking powder
½ teaspoon salt
**½ cup (1 stick/115 g) unsalted
butter, room temperature**
**1½ cups (300 g) granulated
sugar**
2 large eggs
2 large egg yolks
½ teaspoon vanilla extract
½ cup (120 ml) buttermilk
**½ cup (120 ml) honeysuckle
water (see above)**

For the frosting:
3 large egg whites
¼ teaspoon cream of tartar
½ cup (100 g) granulated sugar
**1 cup (240 ml) honeysuckle
syrup (see above)**

To make the honeysuckle water and syrup: Place the honeysuckle
in a bowl and pour over just enough boiling water to cover the
blossoms. Cover the bowl, allow to cool, then refrigerate overnight
or for up to 24 hours.

After steeping the flowers (they will look totally gross and
brown, but smell amazing), strain the liquid into a large bowl,
discarding the blossoms. Reserve ½ cup (120 ml) of this honeysuckle
water for the cake. Measure the remaining liquid and pour it into a
large saucepan. For each cup (240 ml) of honeysuckle water, add
1 cup (200 g) sugar. Bring the mixture to a boil over medium-high
heat and simmer until the sugar is dissolved, about 3 minutes.
Remove it from the heat and let cool. Set aside 1 cup (240 ml) of the
syrup for the frosting. The remaining syrup can be refrigerated for
up to 2 weeks.

To make the cake: Preheat the oven to 350°F (175°C). Butter two
6-inch (15-cm) round cake pans.

In a medium bowl, whisk together the flour, baking powder,
and salt.

In the bowl of an electric mixer fitted with the paddle attachment, cream together the butter and sugar until light and fluffy, 3
to 5 minutes. Add the eggs and yolks one at a time, scraping down
the sides of the bowl after each addition. Stir in the vanilla.

In a small bowl, stir together the buttermilk and honeysuckle
water. Alternate adding the flour mixture and milk mixture to the
egg mixture, beginning and ending with the flour.

Divide batter evenly between the prepared pans. Bake for 25
to 30 minutes, until a toothpick inserted in the center comes out
clean. Allow the layers to cool for 10 minutes in the pans before
turning them out onto a wire rack.

To make the frosting: In the bowl of an electric mixer fitted with the whisk attachment, whip the egg whites and cream of tartar until soft peaks form. Slowly add the sugar and whip until firm peaks form.

In a medium saucepan, bring the honeysuckle syrup to a boil over medium-high heat. Boil until a candy thermometer reads 248°F (120°C).

Begin beating the egg whites again and slowly pour in the boiling honeysuckle syrup in a slow stream. Beat until stiff peaks have formed and the frosting has cooled.

To assemble the cake: Place a cake layer on a plate and spread frosting on top, then cover it with the remaining layer. Cover the outside of the cake with the remaining frosting.

Rhubarb-Ginger
ICE CREAM ROLL

SERVES 10

Tart rhubarb is most often paired with something sweet, like
strawberries, but it's equally tasty with spicy ginger. This roll
can be served immediately or frozen for up to 1 month.

For the filling:
**1 pound (455 g) fresh rhubarb,
stems only, cut into ½-inch
(12-mm) pieces**
**1 teaspoon finely grated fresh
ginger**
½ cup (100 g) granulated sugar

For the cake and assembly:
**½ cup butter (1 stick/115 g)
unsalted butter, softened,
plus more for the pan**
Powdered sugar, for dusting
⅔ cup (85 g) all-purpose flour
¼ teaspoon salt
2 large eggs
2 large egg yolks
½ cup (100 g) granulated sugar
**2 (1-pint/475-ml) containers
vanilla ice cream, softened**

To make the filling: In a medium saucepan, combine the rhubarb,
ginger, and sugar. Bring the mixture to a simmer over medium
heat and allow it to cook until the rhubarb is soft and the liquid
has thickened slightly, about 8 minutes. Remove from the heat and
allow to cool.

To make the cake: Preheat the oven to 350°F (175°C). Butter a
10-by-15-inch (25-by-38-cm) jelly-roll pan. Line the bottom with
parchment paper and butter the paper. Lay a clean kitchen towel
out on your work surface and sprinkle it with powdered sugar so
the cake won't stick.
In a medium bowl, whisk together the flour and salt.
In a heatproof bowl, over a pot of simmering water, combine
the eggs, egg yolks, and sugar. Whisk until the mixture is warmed
through and the sugar has dissolved. Transfer the mixture to the
bowl of an electric mixer fitted with the whisk attachment and beat
until it's pale and thick, about 5 minutes. Gently stir in the flour
and butter.
Pour the batter into the prepared pan and bake until a
toothpick inserted in the center comes out clean, about 15 minutes.
Immediately run a knife around the edges of the pan to loosen
the cake. Turn the cake out onto the prepared kitchen towel,
leaving the paper on. Fold the sides of the towel over the cake, and
roll the cake up in the towel. Allow the cake to cool completely,
seam-side down.

To assemble the roll: Unroll the cake and peel off the paper. Spread
the rhubarb filling evenly over the top. Cover it with the ice cream.
Roll up the cake and place it on a plate, seam-side down, then trim
the ends. Dust the cake with powdered sugar just before serving.

Rhubarb
KUCHEN

SERVES 8

Kuchen is the German version of coffee cake, a lightly sweet yeasted dough covered with fresh fruit and a streusel. I like it with rhubarb, but it would be great with cherries or plums too.

To make the dough: In a small bowl, combine the yeast and warm water and let the mixture stand until foamy, about 5 minutes.

In the bowl of an electric mixer fitted with the whisk attachment, combine the flour, sugar, and salt. Add in the yeast, milk, eggs, vanilla, and almond extract, beating until smooth. Add in the butter and beat until the batter is silky and smooth.

Scrape down the sides of the bowl, then cover it with a kitchen towel and allow the dough to rise about 1 hour, or until doubled in size.

To make the filling: Combine the rhubarb, lemon zest, and brown sugar in a small bowl and set aside.

To make the streusel: Combine the flour, salt, brown sugar, and butter in the bowl of a food processor and pulse until clumps form. Set aside.

To assemble the kuchen: Butter an 8-inch (20-cm) square baking pan. Punch down the dough, then spread it evenly into the prepared pan. Cover it with the rhubarb filling, then the streusel, and allow the dough to rise for 30 minutes.

Meanwhile, preheat the oven to 375°F (190°C).

Bake until a toothpick inserted in the center comes out clean, 30 to 35 minutes. Allow it to cool completely in the pan before serving.

For the dough:
- **1 package (2¼ teaspoons/10 g) active dry yeast**
- **¼ cup (60 ml) warm water (approximately 110°F/45°C)**
- **2¼ cups (285 g) all-purpose flour**
- **⅔ cup (130 g) granulated sugar**
- **½ teaspoon salt**
- **½ cup (120 ml) warm milk (approximately 110°F/45°C)**
- **2 large eggs**
- **1 teaspoon vanilla extract**
- **1 teaspoon almond extract**
- **6 tablespoons (¾ stick/85 g) unsalted butter, softened**

For the filling:
- **½ pound (225 g) rhubarb, stems only, cut into ½-inch (12-mm) pieces**
- **Zest of 1 lemon**
- **3 tablespoons packed light brown sugar**

For the streusel:
- **1 cup (130 g) all-purpose flour**
- **¼ teaspoon salt**
- **½ cup (110 g) packed light brown sugar**
- **4 tablespoons (55 g) unsalted butter, room temperature**

SPINACH CAKE

SERVES 8

A savory cake might be unexpected in the company
of these desserts, but this one is so good I just had to
include the recipe. I like to serve it for a simple Sunday
brunch, with a dollop of crème fraîche or a drizzle of
honey on top and a big salad on the side.

Preheat the oven to 350°F (175°C). Butter a 9-inch (23-cm) round cake pan.

In a large bowl, whisk together the flour, baking powder, baking soda, salt, and pepper.

In a medium bowl, whisk together the eggs, yogurt, and oil. Stir the egg mixture into the flour mixture. Stir in the spinach, walnuts, cherries, and feta.

Spread the batter into the prepared pan and bake until a toothpick inserted in the center comes out clean, 25 to 30 minutes. Allow it to cool slightly and top with crème fraîche to serve.

1½ cups (170 g) all-purpose
   flour
1 teaspoon baking powder
1 teaspoon baking soda
½ teaspoon salt
½ teaspoon freshly ground
   black pepper
2 large eggs
½ cup (120 ml) plain Greek
   yogurt
⅓ cup (75 ml) olive oil
1 cup (30 g) packed baby
   spinach leaves
½ cup (50 g) walnuts, toasted
   and chopped
½ cup (80 g) dried cherries
½ cup (60 g) feta cheese
Crème fraîche, for serving

SUMMER

Blackberry, Peach
& BASIL TRIFLE

SERVES 10

Trifles have always felt like summer to me—even the name
evokes a lazy warm afternoon. I like to make these in little
glass cups and serve them with sweet tea or lemonade.

For the topping and assembly:

**3 large peaches, peeled (if you'd
like) and sliced into ½-inch
(12-mm) pieces**
¼ cup (50 g) granulated sugar
**3 cups (300 g) fresh
blackberries**
1 bunch basil, roughly chopped

For the cake:

**1¼ cups (160 g) all-purpose
flour**
½ cup (70 g) yellow cornmeal
1½ teaspoons baking powder
1 teaspoon baking soda
½ teaspoon salt
**¾ cup (1½ sticks/170 g)
unsalted butter, room
temperature**
1 cup (200 g) granulated sugar
2 large eggs
1 teaspoon vanilla extract
½ cup (120 ml) buttermilk

For the whipped cream

2 cups (480 ml) heavy cream
3 tablespoons powdered sugar
1 teaspoon vanilla extract

To make the topping: In a small bowl, combine the peaches and
2 tablespoons of the sugar. In another small bowl, combine the
blackberries and the remaining 2 tablespoons sugar. Place the fruit
in the refrigerator.

To make the cake: Preheat the oven to 350°F (175°C). Butter a
9-by-5-inch (23-by-12-cm) loaf pan.

In a medium bowl, whisk together the flour, cornmeal, baking
powder, baking soda, and salt.

In the bowl of an electric mixer fitted with the paddle attachment, cream the butter and sugar until light and fluffy, 3 to 5
minutes. Add the eggs one at a time, scraping down the sides of
the bowl after each addition. Beat in the vanilla. Alternate adding
the flour mixture and buttermilk to the mixer bowl, beginning and
ending with the flour.

Pour the batter into the prepared pan and bake until a
toothpick inserted in the center comes out clean, 45 to 50 minutes.
Allow the cake to cool completely and then cut it into cubes.

To make the whipped cream: In a chilled bowl, combine the cream,
powdered sugar, and vanilla. Using a chilled whisk, whip by hand or
with an electric mixer until soft peaks form.

To assemble the trifle: For a single large trifle, scatter half of the
cake cubes in the bottom of a trifle bowl. Spoon over one-third of
the blackberries (along with juices) and a third of the peach slices.
Sprinkle one-third of the basil on top of the peaches. Top with half
of the whipped cream. Repeat the layering process, then top the
trifle with the remaining blackberries, peaches, and basil leaves.

To make individual trifles, fill the bottom of each serving glass
with cubes of cake, add blackberries, peaches, and basil, top with
whipped cream, and garnish with the remaining blackberries,
peaches, and basil leaves.

BLACKBERRY-THYME CAKE

with Honey Goat Cheese Frosting

SERVES 8

In late July my sister and I brave the thorny blackberry bushes
in our backyard and are rewarded with baskets full of ripe
berries. When we've had our fill of eating them by the handful,
I like to use up whatever is left by making this cake.

To make the cake: In a small bowl, stir together the blackberries,
honey, and thyme.

Preheat the oven to 350°F (175°C). Butter two 6-inch (15-cm)
round cake pans.

In a medium bowl, whisk together the flour, baking powder,
baking soda, and salt.

In the bowl of an electric mixer fitted with the paddle
attachment, cream together the butter and sugar until light and
fluffy, 3 to 5 minutes. Add the eggs one at a time, scraping down
the sides of the bowl after each addition. Add the vanilla.

Alternate adding the flour mixture and the buttermilk to the
mixer bowl, beginning and ending with the flour.

Divide the batter evenly between the prepared pans, and top
each with 1 cup of the blackberry mixture.

Bake for 25 to 30 minutes, until a toothpick inserted in the
center comes out clean. Allow to cool for 10 minutes in the pans
before turning the layers out onto a wire rack to cool completely.

To make the frosting: In the bowl of an electric mixer fitted with
the paddle attachment, cream the goat cheese and cream cheese
until light and fluffy, 3 to 5 minutes. Beat in the honey. Reduce the
speed and add the powdered sugar ½ cup (50 g) at a time.

To assemble the cake: Place one cake layer on a plate and spread
the top with frosting, then add the remaining blackberry mixture.
Set the remaining cake layer on top and cover the outside of the
cake with frosting. Top with fresh blackberries and thyme.

For the cake and assembly:

**3 cups (300 g) fresh
blackberries, plus more for
garnishing**

¼ cup (60 ml) honey

**1 teaspoon thyme leaves, plus
more for garnishing**

**1⅔ cups (215 g) all-purpose
flour**

1 teaspoon baking powder

1 teaspoon baking soda

½ teaspoon salt

**½ cup (1 stick/115 g) unsalted
butter, room temperature**

1 cup (200 g) granulated sugar

2 large eggs

1 teaspoon vanilla extract

½ cup (120 ml) buttermilk

For the frosting:

**4 ounces (115 g) goat cheese,
room temperature**

**4 ounces (115 g) cream cheese,
room temperature**

⅓ cup (75 ml) honey

**About 2 cups (200 g) powdered
sugar**

Blackberry, Plum &
HAZELNUT COFFEE CAKE

SERVES 8

When I've got a hankering to bake (which is all the time) but don't know what to make, I'm always drawn toward coffee cakes. They're simple and versatile, and there are so many fruit combinations to try. Blackberry and plum are particularly good together, and I like the hazelnuts for crunch.

For the topping:
- 1 cup (130 g) all-purpose flour
- ½ teaspoon ground cinnamon
- ¼ teaspoon salt
- ½ cup (110 g) packed light brown sugar
- ½ cup (70 g) hazelnuts, roughly chopped
- ½ cup (1 stick/115 g) unsalted butter, melted

For the cake:
- 1½ cups (170 g) all-purpose flour
- 1½ teaspoons baking powder
- ½ teaspoon salt
- ½ cup (1 stick/115 g) unsalted butter, room temperature
- 1 cup (220 g) packed light brown sugar
- 2 large eggs
- 1 teaspoon vanilla extract
- 3 to 4 plums, sliced into ½-inch (12-mm) pieces
- 1 cup (100 g) fresh blackberries

To make the topping: In a medium bowl, combine the flour, cinnamon, salt, brown sugar, and hazelnuts. Pour the melted butter over the mixture and stir until clumps form. Place the topping in the freezer until ready to use.

To make the cake: Preheat the oven to 350°F (175°C). Butter an 8-inch (20-cm) square baking pan.

In a medium bowl, whisk together the flour, baking powder, and salt.

In the bowl of an electric mixer fitted with the paddle attachment, cream the butter and brown sugar until light and fluffy, 3 to 5 minutes. Add the eggs one at a time, scraping down the sides of the bowl after each addition. Beat in the vanilla. Add the flour mixture to the bowl and mix until just combined.

Spread the batter into the prepared pan and arrange the plums and blackberries on top. Pour the topping over the fruit and bake for 45 to 50 minutes, until a toothpick inserted in the center comes out clean. Allow it to cool for 10 minutes and serve warm.

Peach & Raspberry
PAVLOVA

SERVES 6

This pavlova is a play on the famous dessert
Peach Melba. I've swapped out the traditional vanilla
ice cream for a light and airy meringue.

For the topping and assembly:
2 cups (200 g) fresh raspberries
¼ cup (50 g) granulated sugar
2 large, ripe peaches, sliced
   into ½-inch (12-mm) pieces

For the pavlova:
4 large egg whites, room
   temperature
½ teaspoon cream of tartar
Pinch of salt
1 teaspoon vanilla extract
1 cup (200 g) granulated sugar

For the whipped cream:
1 cup (240 ml) heavy cream
2 tablespoons powdered sugar

To make the topping: In a small saucepan, combine half of the raspberries with the sugar. Bring the mixture to a boil over medium-high heat then reduce to a simmer, and cook until the raspberries are soft and the sauce has thickened slightly. Press the sauce through a fine-mesh sieve. Allow it to cool.

To make the pavlova: Preheat the oven to 275°F (135°C). Line a baking sheet with parchment paper. Trace a 9-inch (23-cm) circle on the parchment, using a cake pan as a guide. Flip the parchment over.

In the bowl of an electric mixer fitted with the whisk attachment, beat the egg whites, cream of tartar, and salt at a low-medium speed until soft peaks form. Stir in the vanilla.

Slowly add ½ cup (100 g) of the sugar and increase the speed to medium-high, beating until the meringue holds stiff, glossy peaks.

Add the sugar and beat until very stiff peaks form, 5 to 7 minutes.

Using a spatula, mound the meringue onto the center of the parchment circle. Gently spread it into a round, using the circle as a guide.

Put the baking sheet in the oven and immediately reduce the temperature to 250°F (120°C). Bake the meringue for 1 hour, or until it is dry to the touch and sounds hollow when tapped. Turn off the oven and leave the pavlova inside, allowing it to cool completely.

To make the whipped cream: Combine the cream and powdered sugar in a chilled bowl and, using a chilled whisk, whip by hand or with an electric mixer until soft peaks form.

To assemble the pavlova: Spread the whipped cream onto the cooled meringue. Top the pavlova with the raspberry sauce, the remaining fresh raspberries, and the peaches.

Berry
TRES LECHES CAKE

SERVES 8

I know some folks are hard-core *tres leches* cake lovers, but I've always found it a little bland on its own. I make mine with lime-infused whipped cream, handfuls of berries, and cool mint to give it some bite.

To make the cake: Preheat the oven to 350°F (175°C). Butter an 8-inch (20-cm) square baking pan.

In a medium bowl, whisk together the flour, baking powder, and salt.

In the bowl of an electric mixer fitted with the paddle attachment, beat the eggs, sugar, and vanilla until pale and smooth, 1 to 2 minutes. Alternate adding the flour mixture and butter to the mixer bowl, mixing until just combined.

Pour the batter into the prepared pan and bake until a toothpick inserted in the center comes out clean, 25 to 30 minutes.

To make the milk topping: While the cake is baking, in a medium bowl, mix together the condensed milk, coconut milk, and whole milk.

When the cake comes out of the oven, poke it all over with a skewer and pour the milk mixture slowly over the top. Allow the cake to cool completely.

To make the whipped cream and assemble: In a chilled bowl, combine the cream, powdered sugar, and lime zest. Using a chilled whisk, whip by hand or with an electric mixer until soft peaks form.

Spread the whipped cream over the top of the cake and top it with the berries and fresh mint.

For the cake:

1½ cups (170 g) all-purpose flour
1 teaspoon baking powder
½ teaspoon salt
4 large eggs
1 cup (200 g) granulated sugar
1 teaspoon vanilla extract
½ cup (1 stick/115 g) unsalted butter, melted

For the milk topping:

1 (14-ounce/420-ml) can sweetened condensed milk
1 cup (240 ml) coconut milk
½ cup (120 ml) whole milk

For the whipped cream and assembly:

1 cup (240 ml) heavy whipping cream
¼ cup (25 g) powdered sugar
Zest of 1 lime
1 cup (100 g) fresh blackberries
1 cup (100 g) fresh raspberries
1 cup (100 g) fresh blueberries
Fresh mint leaves

Lavender-Blueberry
CUPCAKES

MAKES 12

These cupcakes remind me of warm afternoons in my garden, eating handfuls of fresh blueberries with the scent of lavender on the breeze.

For the compote:

1 cup (100 grams) blueberries, plus more for garnishing (optional)

3 tablespoons granulated sugar

For the cupcakes:

½ cup (120 ml) whole milk

2 teaspoons dried lavender, plus more for garnishing (optional)

1 cup (130 g) all-purpose flour

1 cup (140 g) cake flour

1½ teaspoons baking powder

¼ teaspoon salt

½ cup (1 stick/115 g) unsalted butter

1 cup (200 g) granulated sugar

2 large eggs

1 teaspoon vanilla extract

1 cup (100 g) fresh blueberries

For the frosting and assembly:

½ cup (1 stick/115 g) unsalted butter, room temperature

1 (8-ounce/226-g) package cream cheese, room temperature

3 tablespoons (45 ml) blueberry compote (see above)

3 cups (300 g) powdered sugar

To make the compote: In a small saucepan, combine the blueberries, sugar, and 1 tablespoon water. Simmer over medium heat, stirring often, until the berries burst and the liquid thickens, about 7 minutes. Set aside to cool.

To make the cupcakes: In a small saucepan, heat the milk over medium-high heat until just boiling. Remove it from the heat and stir in the lavender and steep for 30 minutes. Pour the milk through a fine-mesh sieve to remove the lavender and discard it; reserve the milk.

Preheat the oven to 350°F (175°C). Line a cupcake pan with paper liners.

In a medium bowl, whisk together the all-purpose flour, cake flour, baking powder, and salt.

In the bowl of an electric mixer fitted with the paddle attachment, cream together the butter and sugar until light and fluffy, 3 to 5 minutes. Add the eggs one at a time, scraping down the sides of the bowl after each addition. Add the vanilla.

With the mixer speed on low, add half the flour mixture. Add the milk, then the rest of the flour. Beat until just combined. Gently fold in the blueberries.

Divide the batter evenly among the paper liners, filling each two-thirds full. Bake for 17 to 20 minutes, until a toothpick inserted in the center comes out clean. Allow the cupcakes to cool.

To make the frosting: In the bowl of an electric mixer fitted with the paddle attachment, beat the butter and cream cheese until smooth, about 3 minutes. Add the compote and mix well. Add the powdered sugar, 1 cup (100 g) at a time, beating until smooth.

To assemble the cupcakes: Frost the cupcakes and top each one with a spoonful of compote, a fresh blueberry, or a sprinkling of lavender.

Blueberry & Roasted Peach
ICE CREAM CAKE
SERVES 8

Memories of my childhood birthdays, deep in the dog days of summer, always include the sticky-faced joy that comes from an ice cream cake. I still love them to this day, even if my current version is a little more grown up—vanilla ice cream with blueberry compote and topped with syrupy roasted peaches.

To make the peaches: Preheat the oven to 400°F (205°C).

In a medium bowl, stir together the peaches, brown sugar, ginger, and oil.

Arrange the peaches on a baking sheet and roast until they are tender, 15 to 20 minutes. Allow them to cool completely.

To make the crust: In a medium bowl, combine the pecans, graham cracker crumbs, brown sugar, and butter. Press the mixture into the bottom of a 9-inch (23-cm) springform pan.

To make the compote: In a small saucepan, combine two-thirds of the blueberries with the sugar and ⅓ cup (75 ml) water. Simmer over medium heat until the berries burst, about 10 minutes. Add the remaining third of the blueberries and cook for 8 minutes more, until the compote coats the back of a spoon. Remove from the heat and allow to cool completely.

To make the whipped cream and assemble: Spread half of the ice cream into the prepared crust, then layer on the cooled blueberry compote. Top the compote with the remaining ice cream and smooth the surface. Place in the freezer for 1 hour.

In a chilled bowl, combine the cream, powdered sugar, and vanilla. Using a chilled whisk, whip by hand or with an electric mixer until soft peaks form.

Top the cake with the peaches, blueberries, and whipped cream.

For the peaches:

3 medium peaches, peeled and sliced into ½-inch (12-mm) pieces
3 tablespoons packed light brown sugar
½ teaspoon ground ginger
1 tablespoon vegetable oil

For the crust:

½ cup (50 g) pecan halves, finely chopped
1½ cups (130 g) graham cracker crumbs (from about 12 sheets of crackers)
2 tablespoons packed light brown sugar
4 tablespoons (55 g) unsalted butter, melted

For the compote:

1½ cups (150 g) fresh blueberries
⅓ cup (65 g) granulated sugar

For the whipped cream and assembly:

1 quart (960 ml) vanilla ice cream, softened
1 cup (240 ml) heavy cream
3 tablespoons powdered sugar
1 teaspoon vanilla extract
½ cup (50 g) fresh blueberries

Blueberry-Corn
SKILLET CAKE

SERVES 8

There's nothing like fresh corn—straight off the cob—in the summer. While it might seem an odd combination, I assure you the crunch of the kernels works perfectly with blueberries in this lightly sweet skillet cake. Top it off with jammy compote and you've got a perfect dessert for a hot evening on the porch.

For the cake:
¾ cup (105 g) fine-ground yellow cornmeal
¾ cup (90 g) all-purpose flour
¾ cup (150 g) granulated sugar
1 teaspoon baking powder
¼ teaspoon salt
¾ cup (180 ml) buttermilk
5 tablespoons (70 g) unsalted butter, melted
1 large egg
½ cup (80 g) fresh corn kernels
½ cup (50 g) fresh blueberries

For the compote:
2 cups (200 g) fresh blueberries
⅓ cup (65 g) granulated sugar

To make the cake: Preheat the oven to 350°F (175°C). Butter a 9-inch (23-cm) cast-iron skillet.

In a medium bowl, whisk together the cornmeal, flour, sugar, baking powder, and salt.

In a small bowl, whisk together the buttermilk, butter, and egg. Pour the buttermilk mixture into the flour mixture and stir until just combined. Stir in the corn and blueberries.

Pour the batter into the prepared pan. Bake for 30 to 35 minutes, until a toothpick inserted in the center comes out clean. Allow it to cool slightly.

To make the compote: In a small saucepan, combine half of the blueberries with the sugar and ⅓ cup (75 ml) water. Simmer over medium heat until the berries burst, about 10 minutes. Add the remaining blueberries and cook for 8 minutes more, until the compote coats the back of a spoon. Remove from the heat.

Serve the cake with warm compote.

Dark Chocolate-Raspberry
LAYER CAKE
SERVES 8

Whipped ganache frosting is a dream—lighter and more mousse-like than buttercream and so simple to make.

To make the raspberry filling: In a medium saucepan, combine the raspberries and sugar. Simmer over medium heat until the sugar dissolves and the liquid thickens, about 10 minutes. Remove from the heat and allow to cool.

To make the cake: Preheat the oven to 350°F (175°C). Butter two 9-inch (23-cm) round cake pans and line them with parchment.

In a medium bowl, whisk together the flour, baking powder, and salt.

In another medium bowl, whisk together the egg whites, milk, and vanilla.

In the bowl of an electric mixer fitted with the paddle attachment, cream the butter and sugar until light and fluffy, 3 to 5 minutes. Alternate adding the flour and egg mixtures to the mixer bowl, beginning and ending with the flour.

Pour the batter into the prepared pans and bake until a toothpick inserted in the center comes out clean, 25 to 30 minutes. Allow the layers to cool for 10 minutes before turning them out onto a wire rack.

To make the ganache: Place the chocolate in a medium heatproof bowl. Pour the cream into a small saucepan and bring it to a boil over medium-high heat. Pour the hot cream over the chocolate and let stand for 5 minutes, then whisk until smooth. Allow it to cool to room temperature, about 1 hour.

In the bowl of an electric mixer fitted with the whisk attachment, beat the ganache until fluffy, 3 to 5 minutes.

To assemble the cake: Place one cake layer on a plate and spread it with raspberry filling. Set the remaining layer on top and frost the outside of the cake with the ganache.

For the raspberry filling:
1½ cups (150 g) fresh raspberries
¼ cup (50 g) granulated sugar

For the cake:
2¼ cups (315 g) cake flour
2 teaspoons baking powder
½ teaspoon salt
6 large egg whites
¾ cup (180 ml) whole milk
2 teaspoons vanilla extract
1 cup (2 sticks/225 g) unsalted butter, room temperature
2 cups (400 g) granulated sugar

For the ganache:
12 ounces (340 g) dark chocolate
1½ cups (360 ml) heavy cream

Raspberry
CLAFOUTIS

SERVES 8

Clafoutis is typically served as dessert, but because it's eggy and lightly sweet, I prefer it the next day for breakfast. I've swapped out the traditional unpitted cherries for sweet-tart raspberries, but any summer fruit would do just fine.

3 cups (300 g) fresh raspberries

1 cup (240 ml) whole milk, room temperature

2 tablespoons unsalted butter, melted

½ cup (100 g) granulated sugar

1 teaspoon vanilla extract

4 large eggs

Pinch of salt

¾ cup (90 g) all-purpose flour

Zest of 1 lemon

Powdered sugar, for dusting

Preheat the oven to 450°F (230°C). Butter a 9-inch (23-cm) cast-iron skillet.

Arrange the raspberries in the bottom of the pan in a single layer.

In a food processor, blend the milk, butter, sugar, vanilla, eggs, salt, flour, and lemon zest until smooth.

Pour the batter over the raspberries and bake until a toothpick inserted in the center comes out clean, about 30 minutes.

Allow the clafoutis to cool slightly and top it with powdered sugar before serving.

Heirloom
TOMATO CAKE

SERVES 8

Deep in August, when the tomatoes are practically falling
off the vines and I've had my fill of fresh tomato sandwiches,
gazpacho, and salads, I like to bake up this cake. Nothing beats
the flavorful, homegrown variety of tomatoes found in your
backyard or the local farmers' market.

Squeeze out and discard the juice and seeds from the tomatoes.
Place the tomatoes in a food processor and blend until smooth. Set
aside 1 cup (240 ml) of the puree for the cake and reserve the rest
for another use.

Preheat the oven to 350°F (175°C). Butter a 9-by-5-inch
(23-by-12-cm) loaf pan.

In a medium bowl, whisk together the flour, baking powder,
baking soda, and salt.

In the bowl of an electric mixer fitted with the paddle
attachment, cream the butter and sugar until light and fluffy,
3 to 5 minutes. Add the eggs one at a time, scraping down the
sides of the bowl after each addition. Stir in the orange zest and
ginger. Alternate adding the flour mixture and the reserved
1 cup (240 ml) tomato puree to the mixer bowl, beginning and
ending with the flour.

Pour the batter into the prepared pan and bake until a
toothpick inserted in the center comes out clean, 45 to 50 minutes.
Allow the cake to cool completely before turning out of the pan.

3 to 4 medium heirloom
  tomatoes, halved
1¾ cups (225 g) all-purpose
  flour
1 teaspoon baking powder
½ teaspoon baking soda
½ teaspoon salt
½ cup (1 stick/115 g) unsalted
  butter, room temperature
1 cup (200 g) granulated sugar
2 large eggs
Zest of 1 orange
1 tablespoon freshly grated
  ginger

Peach & Tomato
PRESERVES CAKE
SERVES 8

Peaches are always best eaten whole, juices dripping down your arms, but I do love making jam with them. Combining the peach with acidic tomato balances out the sweetness and is perfect for slathering on top of this simple butter cake.

For the preserves:

2 large Roma tomatoes, roughly chopped
2 medium peaches, peeled and roughly chopped
Juice and zest of 1 lemon
1½ cups (300 g) granulated sugar

For the cake:

1½ cups (170 g) all-purpose flour
1½ teaspoons baking powder
¼ teaspoon salt
½ cup (1 stick/115 g) unsalted butter, room temperature
1 cup (200 g) granulated sugar
2 large eggs, room temperature
1 teaspoon vanilla extract
½ cup (120 ml) whole milk

To make the preserves: In a medium saucepan, combine the tomatoes, peaches, lemon juice and zest, and sugar. Bring the mixture to a boil over medium-high heat, reduce the heat to low, and simmer for 30 to 40 minutes, until the peaches are tender and the mixture has thickened. Pour it into a clean jar and refrigerate it for at least 4 hours.

To make the cake: Preheat the oven to 350°F (175°C). Butter an 8-inch (20-cm) round cake pan.

In a medium bowl, whisk together the flour, baking powder, and salt.

In the bowl of an electric mixer fitted with the paddle attachment, cream the butter and sugar until light and fluffy, about 3 to 5 minutes. Add the eggs one at a time, scraping down the sides of the bowl after each addition. Beat in the vanilla. Alternate adding the flour mixture and the milk to the mixer bowl, beginning and ending with the flour.

Pour the batter into the prepared pan and bake until a toothpick inserted in the center comes out clean, 30 to 35 minutes. Turn out the cake onto a wire rack and allow it to cool completely.

Spread the preserves on top before serving.

Green Tomato
CORNMEAL CAKE

SERVES 8

I grew up eating fried green tomatoes but hadn't tried them in dessert until I was working at a farm-to-table camp one summer. Each morning, the kids and I would pick fresh veggies from the garden and head back into the kitchen, covered in dirt, to bake something with our bounty. One day, we had an abundance of green tomatoes and made a green tomato pie. We were hesitant to try it, but when it was served, everyone sighed with delight. Since then, I've been baking with green tomatoes whenever I can.

Preheat the oven to 350°F (175°C). Butter a 9-inch (23-cm) round cake pan.

Melt 4 tablespoons (55 g) of the butter in a small saucepan over medium heat. Remove from the heat, add the brown sugar and honey, and stir until the sugar is dissolved. Pour the mixture into the prepared pan and arrange the tomato slices on top.

In a large bowl, whisk together the flour, cornmeal, sugar, baking powder, baking soda, and salt.

Melt the remaining ½ cup (115 g) butter, then combine it in a medium bowl with the egg and buttermilk. Whisk the mixture, then pour it into the flour mixture and stir until just combined.

Spread the batter over the tomatoes and bake until a toothpick inserted in the center comes out clean, about 30 minutes.

Let the cake cool in the pan for 15 minutes, then invert it onto a plate.

¾ cup (1½ sticks/170 g) unsalted butter
½ cup (110 g) packed light brown sugar
⅓ cup (75 ml) honey
2 large green tomatoes, thinly sliced
1 cup (130 g) all-purpose flour
½ cup (70 g) fine-ground yellow cornmeal
1 cup (200 g) granulated sugar
1 teaspoon baking powder
½ teaspoon baking soda
½ teaspoon salt
1 large egg
½ cup (120 ml) buttermilk

ROSEMARY CORNMEAL POUND CAKE

with Caramelized Plums

SERVES 8

I grew up eating slices of store-bought pound cake topped
with gooey strawberries. I've tried creating a few variations
on that childhood classic, and this one is the best I've made.
The cornmeal lends a satisfying crunchy texture to the pound
cake, and the caramelized plums are downright dreamy.
(They're delicious over ice cream, too!)

To make the cake: Preheat the oven to 350°F (175°C). Butter a
10-inch (25-cm) tube pan or 10-inch (25-cm) Bundt pan.

In a medium bowl, whisk together the flour, cornmeal, salt, and
rosemary.

In the bowl of an electric mixer fitted with the paddle
attachment, cream the butter and sugar until light and fluffy, 3 to 5
minutes. Add the eggs one at a time, scraping down the sides of the
bowl after each addition. Beat in the vanilla. Alternate adding the
flour mixture and cream to the mixer bowl, beginning and ending
with the flour.

Pour the batter into the prepared pan and bake until a tester
inserted in the center comes out clean, 60 to 65 minutes. Cool the
cake in the pan for 10 minutes before turning it out onto a wire
rack to cool completely.

To make the caramelized plums: In a large skillet, melt the butter
over medium heat. Stir in the brown sugar and salt. When the
sugar has dissolved, add the plums in one layer and cook, turning
them once, until they are tender and golden brown. Remove from
the heat.

Serve each slice of pound cake with a heaping pile of
caramelized plums on top.

For the cake:

2 cups (255 g) all-purpose flour
**1 cup (140 g) fine-ground yellow
cornmeal**
1 teaspoon salt
**2 tablespoons finely chopped
fresh rosemary**
**1 cup (2 sticks/225 g) unsalted
butter, room temperature**
3 cups (600 g) granulated sugar
6 large eggs
2 teaspoons vanilla extract
1 cup (240 ml) heavy cream

For the caramelized plums:

2 tablespoons unsalted butter
**¼ cup (55 g) packed light brown
sugar**
Pinch of salt
**6 or 7 plums, sliced into ½-inch
(12-mm) pieces**

Cantaloupe
MOUSSE CAKE
SERVES 8

This cake is light, airy, and the very definition of refreshing. You could easily swap out the cantaloupe for honeydew or watermelon.

For the crust:

1½ cups (130 g) graham cracker crumbs (from about 12 whole crackers)
2 tablespoons granulated sugar
Zest of 2 limes
Pinch of salt
4 tablespoons (55 g) unsalted butter, melted

For the filling:

¼ cup (28 g) unflavored gelatin
⅓ cup (75 ml) cold water
1 large cantaloupe, seeded and cut into ½-inch (12-mm) chunks
5 large eggs, separated
1½ cups (300 g) granulated sugar
Fresh mint leaves, for garnishing

To make the crust: Preheat the oven to 350°F (175°C). Butter a 9-inch (23-cm) springform pan.

In a large bowl, combine the graham cracker crumbs, sugar, lime zest, salt, and butter. Press the mixture evenly into the bottom of the prepared pan and bake until crisp, 10 to 12 minutes.

To make the filling: In a cup, sprinkle the gelatin over the cold water and let stand until softened, about 5 minutes.

Place the cantaloupe in a blender and process until smooth. You should have about 2½ cups (600 ml) of puree. Pour into a medium saucepan, add the gelatin, and heat over medium, stirring, until the gelatin is dissolved. Remove from the heat.

Fill a large bowl with ice and place a smaller bowl inside it. In a medium bowl, whisk together the egg yolks and 1 cup (200 g) of the sugar. Pour in a third of the hot cantaloupe mixture, whisking constantly, then pour the egg yolk mixture back into the pan with the hot cantaloupe. Cook over medium heat, stirring constantly, until the mixture has thickened, 3 to 4 minutes. Pour it through a fine-mesh sieve into the bowl set in the ice and whisk until the mixture starts to set, 3 to 5 minutes.

In the bowl of an electric mixer fitted with the whisk attachment, whisk the egg whites until soft peaks form. Add the remaining ½ cup (100 g) sugar and whisk until stiff peaks form, about 3 minutes. Fold the egg whites into the melon mixture, making sure they are fully incorporated.

Mound the filling into the prepared crust and refrigerate for at least 2 hours. Garnish with the mint.

CARROT & BEET CUPCAKES

with Beet–Cream Cheese Frosting

MAKES 12

The earthy flavor of the beets makes these little cakes special. That bright pink frosting helps too.

To make the cupcakes: Preheat the oven to 350°F (175°C). Butter a 6-cup muffin pan or six ramekins.

In a large bowl, whisk together the flour, baking powder, baking soda, and salt.

In a medium bowl, whisk together the sugar, oil, eggs, and vanilla. Pour the wet ingredients into the dry mixture and stir until just combined. Stir in the beets and carrots.

Divide the batter among the prepared muffin cups or ramekins and bake until a toothpick inserted in the center comes out clean, 25 to 30 minutes. Transfer the cupcakes to a wire rack and allow them to cool completely.

To make the frosting: In the bowl of an electric mixer fitted with the paddle attachment, beat the cream cheese and butter until creamy and smooth, 3 to 5 minutes. Add the beet and powdered sugar and beat until smooth.

Spread the tops of the cooled cupcakes with frosting.

For the cupcakes:
- **2 cups (255 g) all-purpose flour**
- **1 teaspoon baking powder**
- **½ teaspoon baking soda**
- **½ teaspoon salt**
- **1½ cups (300 g) granulated sugar**
- **¾ cup (180 ml) vegetable oil**
- **3 large eggs**
- **1 teaspoon vanilla extract**
- **1 cup (150 g) finely grated beets**
- **1 cup (90 g) finely grated carrots**

For the frosting:
- **1 ounce (28 g) cream cheese, room temperature**
- **4 tablespoons (55 g) unsalted butter, room temperature**
- **2 tablespoons finely grated beet**
- **1 cup (100 g) powdered sugar**

CARROT CUPCAKES

with Honey Cream Cheese Frosting

MAKES 12

My sister was married on a beautiful day in a garden,
surrounded by herbs, tomato plants, and clucking chickens.
It was simply perfect, and I had the honor of baking these
cupcakes as her wedding cake. The frosting is what makes
these distinctive—the pronounced honey flavor pairs so
well with the spiced carrot cake.

For the cake:

1 cup (110 g) pecan halves, plus
    more for garnishing
2 cups (255 g) all-purpose flour
1 teaspoon baking powder
1 teaspoon baking soda
1 teaspoon salt
1 teaspoon ground cinnamon
1 teaspoon ground ginger
2 cups (440 g) packed dark
    brown sugar
1 cup (240 ml) vegetable oil
4 large eggs
3 cups (270 g) grated carrots

For the frosting:

2 (8-ounce/226-g) packages
    cream cheese, room
    temperature
½ cup (1 stick/115 g) unsalted
    butter, room temperature
⅔ cup (165 ml) honey
1 cup (100 g) powdered sugar

To make the cake: Preheat the oven to 350°F (175°C). Line a
cupcake pan with paper liners.

Spread the pecans in a single layer on a baking sheet and toast
them in the oven just until they become aromatic, about 6 minutes.
Remove them from the pan and roughly chop them.

In a medium bowl, whisk together the flour, baking powder,
baking soda, salt, cinnamon, and ginger.

In the bowl of an electric mixer fitted with the paddle
attachment, beat the brown sugar, oil, and eggs until well blended,
1 to 2 minutes. Add the flour mixture, stirring until just blended.
Stir in the carrots and pecans.

Divide the batter evenly among the paper liners, filling each
about two-thirds full. Bake until a toothpick inserted in the center
comes out clean, about 20 minutes. Transfer the cupcakes to a wire
rack and allow them to cool completely.

To make the frosting: In the bowl of an electric mixer fitted with
the paddle attachment, beat the cream cheese, butter, and honey
until light and fluffy, 3 to 4 minutes. Add the powdered sugar and
beat until smooth.

Frost the cupcakes and press pecan halves or chopped pecans
on top.

ZUCCHINI CHOCOLATE CAKE

with Dark Chocolate Ganache

SERVES 8

After closing my stand at the farmers' market one weekend, I was handed a box full of a friend's leftover zucchini . . . about thirty of them. I was determined to use every last one, and this recipe was by far the best result of that challenge. Despite all the sugar and decadent ganache, the veggies in this cake make it seem a bit virtuous.

To make the cake: Preheat the oven to 350°F (175°C). Butter a 10-inch (25-cm) Bundt pan.

In a medium bowl, whisk together the flour, cocoa powder, baking powder, baking soda, and salt.

In the bowl of an electric mixer fitted with the paddle attachment, cream the butter and sugar until light and fluffy, 3 to 5 minutes. Add the eggs one at a time, scraping the sides of the bowl after each addition. Stir in the vanilla. Alternate adding the flour mixture and milk to the mixer bowl, beginning and ending with the flour. Stir in the zucchini.

Pour the batter into the prepared pan and bake the cake until a tester inserted into the center comes out clean, about 50 minutes. Allow the cake to cool for 10 minutes in the pan before inverting it onto a wire rack to cool completely.

To make the ganache: Place the chocolate in a medium heatproof bowl. Pour the cream into a small saucepan and bring it to a boil over medium-high heat. Pour the hot cream over the chocolate and let it stand for 5 minutes. Whisk until smooth.

Pour the ganache over the cake.

For the cake:

2¼ cups (285 g) all-purpose flour
½ cup (40 g) unsweetened cocoa powder
2 teaspoons baking powder
½ teaspoon baking soda
1 teaspoon salt
1 cup (2 sticks/225 g) unsalted butter, room temperature
1¾ cups (350 g) granulated sugar
2 large eggs
1 teaspoon vanilla extract
½ cup (120 ml) whole milk
2 cups (200 g) finely grated zucchini

For the ganache:

4 ounces (115 g) dark chocolate, at least 60% cocoa, chopped
½ cup (120 ml) heavy cream

Summer Squash &
BANANA CAKE

SERVES 8

If I can grow anything well, it's squash. I always
seem to plant far too much, and I usually have it coming
out of my ears by July. I love sautéing it in a little olive
oil or eating it raw in a salad, but it also adapts well
to baking. I used yellow crookneck squash here, but
any variety would do.

For the cake:

2 cups (255 g) all-purpose flour
1 teaspoon baking powder
½ teaspoon baking soda
½ teaspoon salt
½ teaspoon ground cinnamon
**1½ cups (330 g) packed light
   brown sugar**
¾ cup (180 ml) vegetable oil
3 large eggs
1 teaspoon vanilla extract
**1 cup (100 g) finely grated
   yellow squash**
2 large ripe bananas, mashed

For the frosting:

**1 (8-ounce/226-g) package
   cream cheese, room
   temperature**
**4 tablespoons (55 g) unsalted
   butter, room temperature**
1 teaspoon vanilla extract
1 cup (100 g) powdered sugar

To make the cake: Preheat the oven to 350°F (175°C). Butter a
10-inch (25-cm) round cake pan.

In a medium bowl, combine the flour, baking powder, baking
soda, salt, and cinnamon.

In a large bowl, whisk together the brown sugar, oil, eggs, and
vanilla. Stir in the squash and bananas. Add the dry ingredients
and stir until just combined.

Pour the batter into the prepared pan and bake until a
toothpick inserted in the center comes out clean, about 1 hour.
Turn out onto a wire rack and allow the cake to cool completely.

To make the frosting: In the bowl of an electric mixer fitted with
the paddle attachment, beat the cream cheese and butter until
fluffy and smooth, 3 to 5 minutes. Add the vanilla and powdered
sugar and beat to combine.

Spread the frosting on top of the cake.

PISTACHIO-GINGER SHORTCAKES

with Roasted Apricots

MAKES 6

The combination of ginger and apricot is warm and comforting, perfect for the late days of summer when the evenings turn cool.

To make the apricots: Preheat the oven to 400°F (205°C). Arrange the apricots, cut-side up, on a baking sheet. Sprinkle with the brown sugar and roast until the apricots are tender, 15 to 20 minutes. Remove from the oven and lower the oven temperature to 375°F (190°C).

To make the shortcakes: Grate the butter into a small bowl using the large side of a cheese grater. Stick the grated butter in the freezer for about 20 minutes.

In a large bowl, whisk together the flour, baking powder, salt, sugar, ginger, and pistachios. Add the butter and cut it in with a fork. Add the cream and mix until just combined.

On a floured work surface, pat the dough into a round about ½ inch (12 mm) thick. Using a 3-inch (7.5-cm) biscuit cutter, cut out the shortcakes. Transfer them to a baking sheet, brush the tops with cream, and sprinkle them with sugar. Bake until golden brown, 16 to 18 minutes, and transfer them to a wire rack to cool.

To make the ginger crème fraîche: While the shortcakes are cooling, in a medium bowl, whisk together the crème fraîche, ginger, and honey.

To assemble the shortcakes: Cut the shortcakes in half horizontally and fill them with crème fraîche and apricots; sprinkle with lemon thyme.

For the apricots:

6 apricots, pitted and quartered
¼ cup (55 g) packed light brown sugar

For the shortcakes:

4 tablespoons (55 g) unsalted butter, chilled
1¾ cups (225 g) all-purpose flour
1 tablespoon baking powder
¼ teaspoon salt
2 tablespoons granulated sugar, plus more for sprinkling
½ teaspoon ground ginger
½ cup (65 g) pistachios, roughly chopped
¾ cup (180ml) chilled heavy cream, plus more for brushing tops

For the ginger crème fraîche and assembly:

1 (8-ounce/225-g) container crème fraîche
2 teaspoons finely grated fresh ginger
2 tablespoons honey
1 tablespoon lemon thyme, for garnishing

PEACH BUNDT

with Bourbon-Brown Butter Glaze

SERVES 8

This cake combines two of the best things to come
from the South—peaches and bourbon.

For the cake:

2½ cups (315 g) all-purpose
flour

2 teaspoons baking powder

½ teaspoon baking soda

1 teaspoon salt

1 cup (2 sticks/225 g) unsalted
butter, melted

1½ cups (330 g) packed dark
brown sugar

3 large eggs

1½ teaspoons vanilla extract

3 medium peaches, peeled and
chopped into ½-inch (12-mm)
pieces

For the glaze:

3 tablespoons (45 g) unsalted
butter

1 cup (100 g) powdered sugar

2 tablespoons bourbon

To make the cake: Preheat the oven to 350°F (175°C). Butter a
10-inch (25-cm) Bundt pan.

In a medium bowl, whisk together the flour, baking powder,
baking soda, and salt.

In a large bowl, whisk together the butter, brown sugar, eggs,
and vanilla. Add the flour mixture and stir until just combined.
Stir in the peaches. Pour the batter into the prepared pan and
bake until a tester inserted in the center comes out clean, 50 to 55
minutes. Cool the cake for 10 minutes in the pan before inverting it
onto a wire rack.

To make the glaze: Melt the butter in a small saucepan over
medium heat and cook, stirring occasionally, until it turns golden
brown and nutty scented.

Pour the butter into a medium bowl and whisk in the powdered
sugar and bourbon.

Pour the glaze over the warm cake.

Plum & Apricot
UPSIDE-DOWN CAKE

SERVES 8

I keep a handwritten copy of this recipe in my kitchen and have been tweaking it for years. It originally called for peaches, but I love using sweet-tart fruit like apricots and plums, and will even throw in a few sour cherries on occasion. No matter what fruit you use, always serve this cake warm with a scoop of vanilla ice cream.

Preheat the oven to 350°F (175°C). Butter a 9-inch (23-cm) round cake pan.

Melt the butter in a small saucepan, then add the brown sugar and stir until it is dissolved. Pour the mixture into the prepared pan and arrange the plums and apricots in a single layer on top.

In a small bowl, whisk together the all-purpose flour, hazelnut flour, baking powder, baking soda, and salt.

In the bowl of an electric mixer fitted with the paddle attachment, cream together the butter and granulated sugar until light and fluffy, 3 to 4 minutes. Add the eggs one at a time, scraping down the sides of the bowl after each addition. Beat in the vanilla. Alternate adding the flour mixture and milk to the mixer bowl, beginning and ending with the flour.

Spread the batter over the plums and apricots in the pan and bake until a toothpick inserted in the center comes out clean, about 30 minutes.

Let the cake cool in the pan for 15 minutes, then invert it onto a plate.

4 tablespoons (55 g) unsalted butter
¾ cup (165 g) packed light brown sugar
3 plums, sliced into ½-inch (12-mm) pieces
3 apricots, sliced into ½-inch (12-mm) pieces
1 cup (130 g) all-purpose flour
½ cup (60 g) hazelnut flour
1 teaspoon baking powder
½ teaspoon baking soda
½ teaspoon salt
½ cup (1 stick/115 g) unsalted butter, room temperature
1 cup (200 g) granulated sugar
2 large eggs
1 teaspoon vanilla extract
½ cup (120 ml) whole milk

FALL

Apple Cider
DOUGHNUT CAKE
SERVES 10

My home is surrounded by apple orchards, and each fall I find myself in their little stores, cup of hot mulled cider in my hands, breathing in the scent of freshly fried doughnuts covered in cinnamon sugar. I'm honoring that tradition with this recipe, the cake version of my favorite autumn treat.

3 cups (720 ml) fresh apple cider
2½ cups (315 g) all-purpose flour
2 teaspoons baking powder
1 teaspoon salt
1 teaspoon ground cinnamon
½ teaspoon freshly grated nutmeg
1½ cups (330 g) packed light brown sugar
3 large eggs
¾ cup (1½ sticks/170 g) unsalted butter, melted
1 large Granny Smith apple, peeled, cored, and finely diced
Cinnamon and sugar, for sprinkling

In a medium saucepan, bring the cider to a boil over medium-high heat. Reduce the heat to medium-low and allow the cider to simmer until it is reduced to 1 cup (240 ml), about 25 minutes. Allow it to cool.

Preheat the oven to 350°F (175°C). Butter a 10-inch (25-cm) Bundt pan.

In a large bowl, whisk together the flour, baking powder, salt, cinnamon, and nutmeg.

In a medium bowl, whisk together the brown sugar, eggs, butter, and apple cider. Pour the cider mixture into the flour mixture and stir until just combined. Stir in the apple.

Pour the batter into the prepared pan and bake for 50 to 55 minutes, until a tester inserted in the center comes out clean. Invert the cake onto a wire rack and sprinkle it with cinnamon sugar while still warm.

APPLE-PECAN CAKE

with Apple Cider Caramel

SERVES 8

If you can, visit your local apple orchard to get the freshest, most flavorful apple cider to use in this caramel sauce. It makes all the difference.

To make the apple cider caramel: In a medium saucepan, bring the cider to a boil over medium-high heat, reduce the heat to medium-low, and allow the cider to simmer until it is reduced to ¼ cup (60 ml), about 10 minutes. Add the brown sugar and stir constantly until the sugar dissolves and the syrup is bubbling.

Stop stirring and allow the mixture to boil over medium-high heat, until it turns deep amber (375°F/190°C on a candy thermometer). Remove the pan from the heat and carefully pour in the cream. With a wooden spoon, stir until smooth, then stir in the butter and salt. Allow the caramel to cool.

To make the cake: Preheat the oven to 350°F (175°C). Butter an 8-inch (20-cm) square baking ban.

In a medium bowl, whisk together the flour, baking powder, and salt.

In the bowl of an electric mixer fitted with the paddle attachment, cream the butter and brown sugar until light and fluffy, 3 to 5 minutes. Add the eggs one at a time, scraping down the sides of the bowl after each addition. Add the flour and mix until just combined. Stir in the apples and pecans.

Pour the batter into the prepared pan and bake until a toothpick inserted in the center comes out clean, 35 to 40 minutes. Allow the cake to cool completely in the pan.

To serve, warm the caramel sauce and pour over each slice.

For the apple cider caramel:

- **1 cup (240 ml) fresh apple cider**
- **1 cup (220 g) packed dark brown sugar**
- **½ cup (120 ml) heavy cream, room temperature**
- **1 tablespoon unsalted butter, room temperature**
- **½ teaspoon sea salt**

For the cake:

- **1½ cups (170 g) all-purpose flour**
- **1½ teaspoons baking powder**
- **½ teaspoon salt**
- **¾ cup (1½ sticks/170 g) unsalted butter, room temperature**
- **1½ cups (330 grams) packed dark brown sugar**
- **3 large eggs**
- **2 large apples, peeled, cored, and chopped into ½-inch (12-mm) pieces**
- **1 cup (100 g) pecan halves, toasted and chopped**

APPLE SKILLET CAKE

with Rosemary Crumble

SERVES 8

Apples and rosemary are often paired with pork, but
they work really well in sweet dishes too. I like to
use Honeycrisp apples for this cake as their sweet-tart
flavor distinguishes them from the other varieties.

For the crumble:

1 cup (130 g) all-purpose flour
½ cup (110 g) packed light
    brown sugar
¼ teaspoon salt
4 tablespoons (55 g) unsalted
    butter, room temperature
1 tablespoon roughly chopped
    rosemary

For the cake:

1¾ cups (225 g) all-purpose
    flour
2 teaspoons baking powder
½ teaspoon salt
⅓ cup (75 g) unsalted butter,
    room temperature
1 cup (220 g) packed light
    brown sugar
2 large eggs
1 teaspoon vanilla extract
½ cup (120 ml) whole milk
1 large apple, peeled, cored, and
    diced

To make the crumble: In the bowl of a food processor, combine
the flour, brown sugar, salt, butter, and rosemary and pulse until
clumps form. Place the mixture in the freezer until ready to use.

To make the cake: Preheat the oven to 350°F (175°C). Butter a
9-inch (23-cm) cast-iron skillet.

In a medium bowl, whisk together the flour, baking powder,
and salt.

In the bowl of an electric mixer fitted with the paddle
attachment, cream the butter and brown sugar together until light
and fluffy, 3 to 5 minutes. Add the eggs one at a time, scraping
down the sides of the bowl after each addition. Stir in the vanilla.
Alternate adding the flour mixture and milk to the mixer bowl,
beginning and ending with the flour. Fold in the apples.

Pour the mixture into the prepared pan and sprinkle the
crumble on top.

Bake until a toothpick inserted in the center comes out clean,
40 to 45 minutes. Allow the cake to cool slightly before serving.

Brown Butter
APPLE STACK CAKE

SERVES 8

The stack cake hails from the southern Appalachian Mountains. It was traditionally served as a wedding cake; friends and family would bring the layers, and the bride's family would add the filling. I've switched the traditional dried apple filling and molasses glaze for sautéed apples and spiced whipped cream.

To make the cake: Preheat the oven to 350°F (175°C). Butter three 9-inch (23-cm) round cake pans.

In a medium bowl, whisk together the flour, baking powder, baking soda, and salt.

In the bowl of an electric mixer fitted with the paddle attachment, cream the butter and sugar until light and fluffy, 3 to 5 minutes. Add the eggs one at a time, scraping down the sides of the bowl after each addition. Beat in the vanilla. Alternate adding the flour mixture and milk to the mixer bowl, beginning and ending with the flour. Stir in the pecans.

Divide the batter evenly among the prepared pans. Bake until a toothpick inserted in the center comes out clean, 25 to 30 minutes. Allow the cakes to cool completely in the pans.

To make the filling: While the cakes are cooling, in a large skillet, melt the butter over medium heat, stirring occasionally, until it turns golden brown and nutty scented. Add the brown sugar and apples and cook until the apples are tender, about 5 minutes.

To make the whipped cream: In a chilled bowl, combine the cream, powdered sugar, maple syrup, cinnamon, and ginger. Using a chilled whisk, whip by hand or with an electric mixer until soft peaks form.

To assemble the cake: Transfer one cake layer to a plate and top it with half of the apples. Place the second layer on top and add the remaining apples. Set the remaining cake layer in place, spread whipped cream over the top, and garnish with the pecans.

For the cake:
- **3 cups (385 g) all-purpose flour**
- **1½ teaspoons baking powder**
- **1 teaspoon baking soda**
- **1 teaspoon salt**
- **1 cup (2 sticks/225 g) unsalted butter, room temperature**
- **2 cups (400 g) granulated sugar**
- **3 large eggs**
- **2 teaspoons vanilla extract**
- **1 cup (240 ml) whole milk**
- **1½ cups (150 g) pecan halves**

For the filling:
- **4 tablespoons (55 g) unsalted butter**
- **3 tablespoons packed light brown sugar**
- **3 large apples, cored, and cut into thick slices**

For the whipped cream and assembly:
- **1 cup (240 ml) heavy cream**
- **1 tablespoon powdered sugar**
- **3 tablespoons (45 ml) maple syrup**
- **¼ teaspoon ground cinnamon**
- **¼ teaspoon ground ginger**
- **½ cup (50 g) pecan halves, for garnishing**

Autumn
BREAKFAST CAKE

SERVES 8

When the mornings are just starting to turn
crisp and cool, I love to wrap up with a blanket
and have a slice of this breakfast cake with a
cup of tea on my front porch.

For the cake:
1 cup (130 g) all-purpose flour
1 cup (125 g) whole-wheat flour
1 cup (80 g) old-fashioned oats
1½ teaspoons baking powder
½ teaspoon baking soda
½ teaspoon salt
1 teaspoon ground cinnamon
**½ teaspoon freshly grated
nutmeg**
¼ teaspoon ground cardamom
**1 small pear, peeled, cored,
and finely grated (about 1
cup/110 g)**
**1 small sweet potato, peeled
and finely grated (about 1
cup/110 g)**
**½ cup (1 stick/115 g) unsalted
butter, melted**
**1 cup (220 g) packed light
brown sugar**
1 cup (240 ml) buttermilk
2 large eggs
1 teaspoon vanilla extract
**1 cup (135 g) hazelnuts, toasted
and roughly chopped**

For the whipped cream:
½ cup (120 ml) heavy cream
2 tablespoons powdered sugar
½ teaspoon ground cinnamon

To make the cake: Preheat the oven to 350°F (175°C). Butter a
9-by-5-inch (23-by-12-cm) loaf pan.

In a medium bowl, whisk together both flours, the oats, baking
powder, baking soda, salt, cinnamon, nutmeg, and cardamom.

Place the pear and sweet potato in a large bowl and stir in the
butter, brown sugar, buttermilk, eggs, and vanilla. Pour the wet
ingredients into the flour mixture and stir until just combined. Stir
in ½ cup (70 g) of the hazelnuts.

Pour the batter into the prepared pan and top it with the
remaining hazelnuts. Bake the cake for 45 to 50 minutes, until a
toothpick inserted in the center comes out clean. Allow it to cool
completely in the pan.

To make the whipped cream: Combine the cream, powdered
sugar, and cinnamon in a chilled bowl and, using a chilled whisk,
whip by hand or with an electric mixer until soft peaks form.

Serve the cake with dollops of cinnamon whipped cream.

APPLE CAKE

SERVES 8

When I was a kid, my mom would always say
apple pie was best served with a slice of cheddar cheese.
I thought she was crazy until she finally got me to
try it. This cake is a twist on that idea.

Starting with cheddar biscuit dough patted into the bottom
of a pie plate, it's then filled with apples and covered with
more dough. Almost like a cobbler sandwich.

In a medium bowl, combine the apples, brown sugar, and cinnamon.

Preheat the oven to 375°F (190°C). Butter a 9-inch (23-cm) pie plate.

Grate the butter into a small bowl using the large side of a cheese grater. Stick the grated butter in the freezer for about 20 minutes.

In a large bowl, whisk together the flour, baking powder, salt, and sugar. Add the butter and cut it in with a fork. Pour in the cream, egg, and cheese, and stir until it comes together in a shaggy dough. Knead the dough 5 to 7 times in the bowl, then turn it out onto a floured work surface. Halve the dough and pat half into the bottom of the pie plate.

Spread the apple mixture over the crust and then cover it with the remaining dough. Sprinkle the top with raw sugar. Cut a slit in the top and bake for 40 to 45 minutes, or until the surface of the dough is browned. Allow to cool slightly in the pan before serving.

2 medium apples, peeled, cored, and diced
¼ cup (55 g) packed light brown sugar
½ teaspoon ground cinnamon
½ cup (1 stick/115 g) unsalted butter, cold
2 cups (255 g) all-purpose flour
1½ teaspoons baking powder
½ teaspoon salt
⅓ cup (65 g) granulated sugar
½ cup (120 ml) heavy cream
1 large egg
½ cup (60 g) grated sharp cheddar cheese
Raw sugar, for sprinkling

PUMPKIN ROLL

with Salted Caramel Cream

SERVES 10

This dessert pays homage to the parchment-wrapped slices
of pumpkin roll I get every October from our farm store.

To make the cake: Preheat the oven to 350°F (175°C). Butter a
10-by-15-inch (25-by-38-cm) jelly-roll pan. Line the bottom with
parchment paper and butter the paper. Lay a clean kitchen towel
out on your work surface and dust it with powdered sugar.

In a large bowl, whisk together the flour, granulated sugar,
baking powder, cinnamon, nutmeg, and salt.

In a medium bowl, whisk together the eggs and pumpkin
puree. Pour the egg mixture into the flour mixture and stir.

Pour the batter into the prepared pan and bake until a
toothpick inserted in the center comes out clean, about 15 minutes.

Run a knife around the edges of the pan to loosen the cake.
Turn the cake onto the prepared towel, leaving the paper on. Fold
the sides of the towel over and roll up the cake in the towel. Allow it
to cool, seam-side down.

To make the caramel sauce and filling: In a medium saucepan,
heat the brown sugar and ¼ cup (60 ml) water over medium-high
and stir until the sugar dissolves and the syrup is bubbling. Stop
stirring and allow the caramel to boil until it turns deep amber.
Watch it closely—it burns easily. Remove the pan from the heat and
carefully pour in the cream. With a wooden spoon, stir until the
caramel is smooth. Stir in 1 tablespoon of the butter and the salt.

In the bowl of an electric mixer fitted with the paddle
attachment, beat the cream cheese and remaining 4 tablespoons
(55 g) butter until smooth and creamy, 3 to 5 minutes. Add 1 cup
(240 ml) of the caramel sauce (you might have to reheat it just
slightly so it's pourable, but make sure it's not too hot) and beat to
combine. Add the powdered sugar, ½ cup (50 g) at a time, until the
filling is smooth.

To assemble the cake: Unroll and peel off the paper. Spread the
filling over the cake. Roll up the cake and place it seam-side down;
trim the ends. Top with powdered sugar and caramel sauce.

For the cake:

Powdered sugar, for dusting
¾ cup (90 g) all-purpose flour
1 cup (200 g) granulated sugar
1 teaspoon baking powder
1 teaspoon ground cinnamon
½ teaspoon freshly grated nutmeg
¼ teaspoon salt
3 large eggs
⅔ cup (165 g) canned pumpkin puree

For the caramel sauce and filling:

1 cup (220 g) packed light brown sugar
½ cup (120 ml) heavy cream, room temperature
5 tablespoons (70 g) unsalted butter, room temperature
1 teaspoon sea salt
1 (8-ounce/226-g) package cream cheese, room temperature
2 cups (200 g) powdered sugar, plus more for dusting

SPICED PUMPKIN CUPCAKES

with Bourbon Buttercream

MAKES 12

The scent of these spiced cupcakes wafting through your kitchen on a chilly day is the very essence of the season. I've topped them off using a buttercream with a kick—bourbon is a nice contrast to the sweet pumpkin flavor.

For the cupcakes:

2 cups (255 g) all-purpose flour
1½ teaspoons baking powder
½ teaspoon baking soda
¼ teaspoon salt
1 teaspoon ground cinnamon
½ teaspoon ground ginger
½ teaspoon freshly grated nutmeg
¼ teaspoon ground allspice
½ cup (1 stick/115 g) unsalted butter, room temperature
1 cup (220 g) packed dark brown sugar
½ cup (100 g) granulated sugar
1 cup (245 g) canned pumpkin puree
1½ teaspoons vanilla extract
2 large eggs
½ cup (120 ml) buttermilk

For the frosting:

1 cup (2 sticks/225 g) unsalted butter, softened
3 cups (300 g) powdered sugar, sifted
¼ teaspoon salt
3 tablespoons (45 ml) bourbon
1 teaspoon vanilla extract
1 to 2 tablespoons whole milk
Cinnamon and sugar, for sprinkling

To make the cupcakes: Preheat the oven to 350°F (175°C). Line a cupcake pan with paper liners.

In a medium bowl, whisk together the flour, baking powder, baking soda, salt, cinnamon, ginger, nutmeg, and allspice.

In the bowl of an electric mixer fitted with the paddle attachment, beat the butter, brown sugar, and granulated sugar on medium speed until light and fluffy, 4 to 5 minutes. Add the pumpkin puree and vanilla. Add the eggs one at a time, scraping down the sides of the bowl after each addition. Alternate adding the flour mixture and buttermilk to the mixer bowl, beginning and ending with the flour.

Divide the batter evenly among the paper liners, filling each about three-quarters full. Bake until a toothpick inserted into a cupcake center comes out clean, 17 to 20 minutes. Turn out onto a wire rack and allow the cupcakes to cool completely.

To make the frosting: In the bowl of an electric mixer fitted with the paddle attachment, cream the butter until smooth, 2 to 3 minutes. Add in the powdered sugar, salt, bourbon, and vanilla and beat until light and fluffy, adding enough milk to reach the desired consistency.

Top the cupcakes with frosting and a sprinkling of cinnamon sugar.

PUMPKIN CREPE CAKE

with Sweet Potato Caramel Sauce

SERVES 8

*There's something so satisfying about making this cake. Sure,
it takes a lot of time and patience, flipping so many crepes,
but it's all worth it when you're sitting down with a slice and
contemplating the towering layers filled with spiced pastry cream
and topped with sweet potato caramel sauce.*

For the caramel sauce:

**4 pounds (1.8 kg) sweet
potatoes, peeled and roughly
chopped**
¼ cup (50 g) granulated sugar
¼ cup (60 ml) heavy cream
**2 tablespoons unsalted butter,
room temperature**

For the pastry cream:

2 cups (480 ml) whole milk
⅔ cup (130 g) granulated sugar
Pinch of salt
6 large egg yolks
⅓ cup (40 g) all-purpose flour
½ teaspoon ground cinnamon
**¼ teaspoon freshly grated
nutmeg**
**2 tablespoons unsalted butter,
cut into small pieces**

To make the caramel sauce: Preheat the oven to 400°F (205°C).
Place the sweet potatoes and 1 cup (240 ml) water in a 9-by-13-
inch (23-by-33-cm) baking pan. Roast for 55 to 60 minutes or
until the sweet potatoes are tender. Pour the sweet potatoes and
liquid into a cheesecloth-lined strainer set over a large bowl and let
them sit for half an hour. When they have cooled, squeeze them in
the cheesecloth to extract the remaining liquid. Discard the solid
sweet potatoes.

In a medium saucepan, bring the sweet potato liquid and sugar
to a boil over medium-high heat. Reduce the heat to medium-low
and allow the syrup to cook, stirring occasionally, until the liquid
has reduced and thickened. Remove from the heat, stir in the
cream and butter, and allow to cool.

To make the pastry cream: In a medium saucepan, combine the
milk, ⅓ cup (65 g) of the sugar, and the salt. Heat over medium
until the mixture begins to simmer.

In a large bowl, whisk together the egg yolks, flour, cinnamon,
nutmeg, and the remaining ⅓ cup (65 g) sugar. Whisking constantly,
slowly pour ½ cup (120 ml) of the milk mixture into the egg yolks.
When the mixture is combined, pour it back into the saucepan with
the remaining milk mixture and cook, whisking constantly, until
the mixture is thickened. Pour through a fine-mesh sieve into a
bowl. Stir in the butter until it is completely melted. Press plastic
wrap directly on the top and refrigerate until cool.

To make the crepes: Place all the ingredients except the butter in a food processor and blend until smooth.

Melt about 1 teaspoon of the butter in a 10-inch (25-cm) skillet over medium heat. Add ¼ cup (60 ml) of the batter and swirl so the batter covers the pan. Let the crepe cook for about a minute, or until the crepe is set. Flip it and cook for another 30 seconds. Transfer the crepe to a wire rack to cool. Continue until all the crepe batter has been used.

To assemble the cake: Place one crepe on a serving plate and spread a thin layer of pastry cream on top. Lay a second crepe on top and add another layer of pastry cream. Continue until all the remaining crepes and pastry cream have been used. Pour the caramel sauce over the top.

For the crepes:

1½ cups (170 g) all-purpose flour
2 tablespoons granulated sugar
½ teaspoon baking powder
½ teaspoon salt
½ teaspoon ground cinnamon
¼ teaspoon freshly grated nutmeg
¼ teaspoon ground ginger
2 cups (480 ml) whole milk
4 large eggs
1 teaspoon vanilla extract
½ cup (125 g) canned pumpkin puree
3 tablespoons (45 g) unsalted butter, melted

Pumpkin & Apple
RICE PUDDING CAKE

SERVES 8

Pumpkin, apples, cranberries, hazelnuts—this cake
is synonymous with the flavors of fall. Most
of the time, I serve it as an indulgent weekend
breakfast, eaten by a crackling fire.

For the cake:

1 cup (200 g) Arborio rice
3 cups (720 ml) whole milk
**1 cup (220 g) packed light
  brown sugar**
**1 cup (245 g) canned pumpkin
  puree**
1 teaspoon vanilla extract
**1 tablespoon dark unsulfured
  molasses**
1 teaspoon ground cinnamon
½ teaspoon ground ginger
¼ teaspoon salt
3 large eggs

For the topping:

**2 large apples, cored, peeled,
  and diced**
½ cup (50 g) dried cranberries
**¼ cup (55 g) packed light brown
  sugar**
¼ teaspoon ground cinnamon
**½ cup (70 g) hazelnuts, toasted
  and chopped, for garnishing**

To make the cake: In a medium saucepan, combine the rice, milk, and brown sugar and bring the mixture to a boil over medium-high heat. Reduce the heat to medium-low and cook until the rice is tender and the milk is absorbed, about 5 to 7 minutes. Allow to cool completely.

Preheat the oven to 325°F (165°C). Butter a 9-inch (23-cm) springform pan.

In a medium bowl, whisk together the pumpkin puree, vanilla, molasses, cinnamon, ginger, salt, and eggs. Stir the pumpkin mixture into the rice mixture. Pour it into the prepared pan and bake until firm to the touch, 30 to 35 minutes. Cool to room temperature.

To make the topping: In a medium saucepan, combine the apples, cranberries, brown sugar, and cinnamon and heat over medium, stirring occasionally, until the apples are tender, about 20 minutes.

To serve, top each slice with the apple-cranberry compote and sprinkle with hazelnuts.

SWEET POTATO CUPCAKES

with Marshmallow Frosting

MAKES 12

Sweet potato casserole is my favorite thing on the Thanksgiving table. This cupcake is inspired by my family's version—while most recipes call for a sprinkling of pecans or marshmallows, we've always topped our casserole with both.

To make the cupcakes: Preheat the oven to 350°F (175°C). Line a cupcake pan with paper liners.

Place the sweet potatoes in a medium saucepan and cover them with water. Bring to a boil over medium-high heat and cook until the potatoes are tender, about 10 minutes. Drain and puree them in a food processor until smooth. Allow them to cool.

In a large bowl, whisk together the all-purpose flour, cake flour, baking powder, salt, cinnamon, and nutmeg.

In a medium bowl, whisk together the brown sugar, eggs, and sweet potato puree. Whisk in the oil, milk, and vanilla. Pour the sweet potato mixture into the flour mixture and stir until just combined.

Divide the batter evenly among the paper liners, filling each about two-thirds full. Bake for 17 to 20 minutes, until a toothpick inserted in the center comes out clean. Transfer the cupcakes to a wire rack and allow them to cool completely.

To make the frosting: In a heatproof bowl, over a pot of simmering water, combine the egg whites, sugar, salt, and cream of tartar. Whisk until the mixture is warmed through and the sugar has dissolved. Transfer the mixture to the bowl of an electric mixer fitted with the whisk attachment and beat the mixture on high speed until stiff, glossy peaks form, 5 to 7 minutes. Mix in the vanilla.

To assemble the cupcakes: Preheat the broiler. Frost each cupcake and top with a pecan. Place the cupcakes under the broiler for a few minutes, until the frosting is lightly browned.

For cupcakes:
2 large sweet potatoes, peeled and cut into chunks
1 cup (130 g) all-purpose flour
1 cup (140 g) cake flour
1½ teaspoons baking powder
¼ teaspoon salt
1 teaspoon ground cinnamon
½ teaspoon freshly grated nutmeg
1 cup (220 g) packed dark brown sugar
2 large eggs
½ cup (120 ml) vegetable oil
½ cup (120 ml) whole milk
1 teaspoon vanilla extract

For the frosting and assembly:
3 large egg whites
1 cup (200 g) granulated sugar
Pinch of salt
¼ teaspoon cream of tartar
½ teaspoon vanilla extract
12 pecan halves, for topping

SWEET POTATO SAGE CAKE

with Maple Glaze

SERVES 8

The earthy, slightly musky scent and
flavor of sage paired with sweet potato
make this cake something special.

For the cake:

**1 large sweet potato, peeled
  and cut into chunks**
**1½ cups (170 g) all-purpose
  flour**
1 teaspoon baking powder
½ teaspoon baking soda
¼ teaspoon salt
½ teaspoon ground cinnamon
½ teaspoon ground ginger
1 cup (200 g) granulated sugar
3 large eggs
½ cup (120 ml) vegetable oil
2 teaspoons vanilla extract
**1 tablespoon finely chopped
  sage leaves**

For the maple glaze:

⅓ cup (35 g) powdered sugar
2 tablespoons maple syrup

To make the cake: Preheat the oven to 350°F (175°C). Butter a
9-by-5-inch (23-by-12-cm) loaf pan.

Place the sweet potato in a medium saucepan and cover with
water. Bring to a boil over medium-high heat and cook until the
potato is tender, about 10 minutes. Drain it and puree in a food
processor until smooth. Allow the puree to cool.

In a medium bowl, whisk together the flour, baking powder,
baking soda, salt, cinnamon, and ginger.

In a large bowl, whisk together the sugar, eggs, oil, vanilla, and
sweet potato puree. Pour the flour mixture into the sweet potato
mixture and stir until just combined. Stir in the sage.

Pour the batter into the prepared pan and bake for 1 hour, or
until a toothpick inserted in the center comes out clean. Turn out
onto a wire rack and allow to cool slightly.

To make the maple glaze: In a small bowl, whisk together the
powdered sugar and maple syrup until smooth. Pour the glaze over
the warm cake.

BUTTERNUT SQUASH CAKE

with Cinnamon-Walnut Filling

SERVES 8

I like to wrap this hearty cake up in parchment and twine and give it as a gift to friends. It's easy to transport, and everyone loves the gooey cinnamon filling.

Preheat the oven to 350°F (175°C). Butter a 9-by-5-inch (23-by-12-cm) loaf pan.

Place the squash in a medium saucepan and cover with water. Bring to a boil over medium-high heat and cook until the squash is tender, about 10 minutes. Drain it and puree in a food processor until smooth. Allow the puree to cool. Measure out 1 cup (240 ml) of the cooled butternut squash puree and save the remainder for another use.

In a medium bowl, stir together 1 cup (220 g) of the brown sugar, 1½ teaspoons of the cinnamon, the walnuts, and the butter.

In another medium bowl, whisk together the flour, baking powder, salt, remaining 1 teaspoon cinnamon, and the nutmeg.

In a large bowl, whisk together the puree, remaining 1 cup (220 g) brown sugar, eggs, and oil. Pour the flour mixture into the squash mixture and stir to combine.

Pour the batter into the prepared pan, filling it halfway, then sprinkle on the walnut mixture. Cover the nuts with the remaining batter. Bake the cake for 45 to 50 minutes, until a toothpick inserted in the center comes out clean. Allow the cake to cool in the pan for 10 minutes before turning it out onto a wire rack to cool completely.

1 small butternut squash, peeled and cut into chunks
2 cups (440 g) packed brown sugar
2½ teaspoons ground cinnamon
½ cup (50 g) walnuts, chopped
4 tablespoons (55g) unsalted butter, melted
1½ cups (170 g) all-purpose flour
2 teaspoons baking powder
½ teaspoon salt
½ teaspoon freshly grated nutmeg
2 large eggs
¼ cup (60 ml) vegetable oil

SWEET POTATO WHOOPIE PIES

with Molasses Filling

MAKES 12

They're called pies and look like cookies—but they're actually little cakes filled with frosting.

For the cakes:

2 large sweet potatoes, peeled and cut into chunks
3 cups (385 g) all-purpose flour
1 teaspoon baking powder
1 teaspoon baking soda
½ teaspoon salt
2 teaspoon ground cinnamon
1½ teaspoons ground ginger
¼ teaspoon freshly grated nutmeg
2 cups (440 g) packed light brown sugar
1 cup (240 ml) vegetable oil
1 teaspoon vanilla extract
2 large eggs

For the filling:

½ cup (1 stick/115 g) unsalted butter, room temperature
1 (8-ounce/226-g) package cream cheese, room temperature
2 tablespoons dark unsulfured molasses
1 cup (100 g) powdered sugar, plus more for dusting

To make the cakes: Preheat the oven to 350°F (175°C). Butter two large baking sheets.

Place the sweet potatoes in a medium saucepan and cover with water. Bring to a boil over medium-high heat and cook until the potatoes are tender, about 10 minutes. Drain them and puree in a food processor until smooth. Allow the puree to cool.

In a medium bowl, whisk together the flour, baking powder, baking soda, salt, cinnamon, ginger, and nutmeg.

In a large bowl, whisk together the brown sugar, oil, vanilla, and sweet potato puree. Add the eggs one at a time, whisking to combine, then stir in the flour mixture.

Drop scoops of batter, about 2 tablespoons each, onto the prepared baking sheets, placing them about 2 inches (5 cm) apart. You should be able to fit about 6 on each sheet (remember, you need an even number for the assembly). Bake the cakes until a toothpick inserted in the center comes out clean, 12 to 15 minutes total, rotating the baking sheets between the upper and lower oven racks after they've been in for about 6 minutes. Transfer the cakes to a wire rack and allow them to cool completely. Repeat so that you have 24 cakes.

To make the filling: In the bowl of an electric mixer fitted with the paddle attachment, beat the butter and cream cheese until smooth and creamy, 3 to 5 minutes. Beat in the molasses. Reduce the speed and add the powdered sugar, ½ cup (50 g) at a time, and beat until slightly fluffy.

To assemble the whoopie pies: Spread a heaping tablespoon of filling onto the flat side of half the cakes, then top each with another cake to make sandwiches. Dust the sandwiches with powdered sugar before serving.

Roasted Kabocha Squash
CINNAMON ROLL CAKE
with Sage-Maple Glaze
SERVES 8

*I love kabocha squash because it's naturally sweet
and creamy, but if you can't find it, butternut squash
or even pumpkin makes a fair substitute.*

For the dough:
**1 kabocha squash, peeled,
    seeded, and cut into chunks**
**1 package (2¼ teaspoons/10 g)
    active dry yeast**
**¼ cup (60 ml) warm water
    (110°F/45°C)**
3 cups (385 g) all-purpose flour
3 tablespoons granulated sugar
1 teaspoon salt
1 teaspoon ground cinnamon
½ teaspoon ground ginger
**½ cup (120 ml) whole milk,
    room temperature**
**6 tablespoons (¾ stick/85 g)
    unsalted butter, melted**
1 large egg

For the roll assembly:
**¾ cup (165 g) packed light
    brown sugar**
1 tablespoon ground cinnamon
**4 tablespoons (55 g) unsalted
    butter, melted**

For the glaze:
1 cup (100 g) powdered sugar
**2 tablespoons unsalted butter,
    melted**
¼ cup (60 ml) maple syrup
**¼ teaspoon finely chopped
    fresh sage leaves**
Pinch of salt

To make the dough: Place the squash in a medium saucepan and
cover with water. Bring to a boil over medium-high heat and cook
until the squash is tender, about 10 minutes. Drain it and puree in
a food processor until smooth. Allow the puree to cool. Measure
out 1 cup (240 ml) of the cooled puree and save the remainder for
another use.

In a small bowl, combine the yeast and warm water and let the
mixture stand until foamy, about 5 minutes.

In a large bowl, whisk together the flour, sugar, salt, cinnamon,
and ginger.

In the bowl of an electric mixer fitted with the paddle
attachment, combine the yeast mixture, squash puree, milk, butter,
and egg. With the mixer on medium speed, add the flour mixture
about a third at a time, until a soft dough forms. Switch to the
dough hook and knead until the dough is elastic and pulls away
from the sides of the mixer bowl.

Place the dough in a lightly buttered bowl, cover it loosely with
a damp kitchen towel, and allow it to rise until doubled in size,
about 1 hour.

To assemble the roll: In a small bowl, mix the brown sugar and
cinnamon.

Lightly butter a 9-inch (23-cm) cast-iron skillet. On a floured
work surface, roll the dough into a 12-by-18-inch (30.5-by-46-cm)
rectangle. Brush the butter over the dough and sprinkle it with the
cinnamon sugar.

Using a sharp knife, cut the dough crosswise into six 2-inch-
(5-cm-) wide strips. Roll up one strip and place it in the center of
the prepared pan. Continue wrapping dough strips around the first
roll until you have one large cinnamon roll.

Cover the cake with a damp kitchen towel and let it rise until it has again doubled in size, about 1 hour.

Preheat the oven to 350°F (175°C). Bake for 30 to 35 minutes, until lightly browned. Allow the cake to cool slightly.

To make the glaze: While the cake is cooling, in a medium bowl, whisk together the powdered sugar, butter, and maple syrup until smooth. Stir in the sage and salt. Pour the glaze over the warm cake.

Autumn
GRAPE CAKE

SERVES 8

This cake is perfect for the grapes that show up
at farmers' markets in the late fall. Try mixing
different varieties, some sweet and some tart.

Preheat the oven to 350°F (175°C). Butter a 9-inch (23-cm) round cake pan.

In a large bowl, whisk together the all-purpose flour, almond flour, baking powder, and salt.

In another large bowl, whisk together the eggs, sugar, and lemon zest. Whisk in the milk, oil, and butter. Pour the wet mixture into the flour mixture and stir until just combined. Stir in half of the grapes.

Pour the batter into the prepared pan and bake for 15 minutes, then remove it from the oven and scatter the remaining grapes on top. Continue baking until a toothpick inserted in the center comes out clean, an additional 25 to 30 minutes.

Turn the cake out onto a wire rack and allow it to cool completely.

1 cup (130 g) all-purpose flour
¾ cup (105 g) almond flour
1½ teaspoons baking powder
½ teaspoon salt
2 large eggs
¾ cup (150 g) granulated sugar
Zest of 1 lemon
⅓ cup (75 ml) whole milk
¼ cup (60 ml) extra-virgin olive oil
4 tablespoons (55 g) unsalted butter, melted
2 cups (300 g) whole seedless grapes

Whiskey, Pear &
MAPLE CHEESECAKE

SERVES 8

I grew up eating cheesecake at church potlucks. These cakes
were simple affairs, sometimes topped with gooey cherries.
My take on this favorite is made distinctly autumnal with
maple, pear, and a glug of whiskey. It's delicious, although
the church ladies might not approve of the booze.

For the crust:

**2 cups (170 g) graham cracker
crumbs (from about 18 whole
crackers)**

½ teaspoon ground cinnamon

**2 tablespoons packed light
brown sugar**

**6 tablespoons (¾ stick/85 g)
unsalted butter, melted**

For the pear filling:

2 tablespoons unsalted butter

**4 slightly underripe pears,
peeled, cored, and diced**

**3 tablespoons packed dark
brown sugar**

1 tablespoon all-purpose flour

2 tablespoons whiskey

For the cheese filling:

**3 (8-ounce/226-g) packages
cream cheese, softened**

**½ cup (110 g) packed dark
brown sugar**

¼ cup (30 g) all-purpose flour

¼ teaspoon salt

1½ teaspoons vanilla extract

**1½ cups (360 ml) grade-A maple
syrup, boiled until reduced to
1 cup (240 ml) and cooled**

3 large eggs

To make the crust: Preheat the oven to 350°F (175°C). Butter a
10-inch (25-cm) springform pan.

In a medium bowl, combine the graham cracker crumbs,
cinnamon, brown sugar, and butter. Press the mixture evenly into
the pan. Bake until crisp, 10 to 12 minutes.

To make the pear filling: In a large skillet, melt the butter over
medium heat. Add the pears and sprinkle them with brown sugar
and flour. Add the whiskey. Cook until the pears are tender, about 5
minutes. Spread the filling into the prepared crust.

To make the cheese filling: In the bowl of an electric mixer fitted
with the paddle attachment, beat the cream cheese and brown
sugar until smooth. Mix in the flour, salt, and vanilla. Add the
reduced maple syrup. Add the eggs one at a time, scraping down
the sides of the bowl after each addition.

Pour the cheese filling over the pears in the crust and bake for
50 to 55 minutes, until the center is just set.

Allow the cheesecake to cool slightly on a wire rack before
unmolding and transferring it to the refrigerator to cool completely.

Pear & Hazelnut
TORTE

SERVES 8

The toasted, nutty flavor of hazelnut flour combined with sweet pieces of just-ripened pear make for an earthy, beautiful dessert.

Preheat the oven to 350°F (175°C). Butter a 9-inch (23-cm) round cake pan.

In a small bowl, whisk together the hazelnut flour, all-purpose flour, and salt.

In the bowl of an electric mixer fitted with the whisk attachment, whip ½ cup (100 g) of the sugar and the egg yolks until the mixture is thick and pale, about 5 minutes. Add the oil and vanilla, and transfer the mixture to a large bowl. Stir in the flour mixture, followed by the pears.

Clean the electric mixer bowl and fit the machine with the whisk attachment. Add the egg whites and remaining ½ cup (100 g) sugar to the bowl and beat until stiff peaks form, 3 to 5 minutes. Fold the egg whites into the batter.

Pour the mixture into the prepared pan.

Bake the cake for 30 to 35 minutes, until a toothpick inserted in the center comes out clean.

Turn the cake out onto a wire rack and allow it to cool completely.

1 cup (115 g) hazelnut flour
½ cup (55 g) all-purpose flour
½ teaspoon salt
1 cup (200 g) granulated sugar
4 large eggs, separated
¼ cup (60 ml) extra-virgin olive oil
½ teaspoon vanilla extract
1 medium pear, peeled, cored, and chopped into ¼-inch (6-mm) pieces

WINTER

Blood Orange-Glazed
EARL GREY DOUGHNUTS

MAKES 12

In the beginning of the season, I spend as many mornings as possible on my front porch with a cup of tea. So when the cold days of winter arrive and I can't get outside, these doughnuts are the perfect way to recapture that feeling. Earl Grey is full of citrusy flavors, and the blood orange glaze really brings those out.

If you don't have a doughnut pan, these can be made in a muffin pan and baked for 17 to 20 minutes.

To make the doughnuts: In a medium saucepan, bring the milk to a boil over medium-high heat. Remove from the heat and stir in the tea. Cover the pan and allow the mixture to cool completely.

Preheat the oven to 350°F (175°C). Butter two 6-well doughnut pans.

In a large bowl, whisk together the flour, sugar, baking powder, baking soda, salt, and lemon zest.

In a medium bowl, whisk together the eggs, tea milk, and vanilla. Stir the egg mixture and the butter into the flour mixture until just combined.

Pour the batter into a pastry bag (or a plastic bag with a corner snipped off) and fill each doughnut well three-quarters full.

Bake the doughnuts for 12 to 15 minutes, until they are springy to the touch. Turn them out onto a wire rack and allow them to cool completely.

To make the glaze: In a medium bowl, whisk together the powdered sugar, orange juice, orange zest, and butter. Add water to reach the desired consistency if needed.

When the doughnuts have cooled, dip the top of each one in the glaze or drizzle with a spoon. Place the doughnuts on a wire rack set over a baking sheet and let the glaze drip.

For the doughnuts:
1 cup (240 ml) whole milk
1 tablespoon Earl Grey tea leaves (from about 3 tea bags)
2½ cups (315 g) all-purpose flour
1½ cups (300 g) granulated sugar
1 teaspoon baking powder
1 teaspoon baking soda
½ teaspoon salt
Zest of 1 lemon
2 large eggs
1 teaspoon vanilla extract
½ cup (1 stick/115 g) unsalted butter, melted

For the glaze:
1 cup (100 g) powdered sugar
Juice of 1 blood orange
Zest of 2 blood oranges
2 tablespoons unsalted butter, melted

Orange Rose Water
CHIFFON LAYER CAKE
SERVES 8

The rose water and orange in this cake
will transport you to the Middle East
with one whiff.

For the cake:
2¼ cups (315 g) cake flour
**1½ cups (300 g) granulated
  sugar**
1 tablespoon baking powder
½ teaspoon ground cardamom
1 teaspoon salt
½ cup (120 ml) vegetable oil
7 large eggs, separated
**Zest and juice of 2 or 3
  oranges (enough to make
  ½ cup/120 ml juice)**
½ teaspoon cream of tartar

For the whipped cream:
2 cups (480 ml) heavy cream
1 tablespoon powdered sugar
2 tablespoons honey
**2 to 3 teaspoons rose water
  (to taste)**

For the assembly:
½ cup (65 g) salted pistachios
Orange zest, for sprinkling

To make the cake: Preheat the oven to 325°F (165°C). Line three
9-inch (23-cm) round cake pans with parchment.

In a large bowl, whisk together the flour, sugar, baking powder,
cardamom, and salt.

In a medium bowl, whisk together the oil, egg yolks, orange
zest and juice, and ½ cup (120 ml) water. Add the wet mixture to
the flour mixture and stir until just combined.

In the bowl of an electric mixer fitted with the whisk
attachment, beat the egg whites and cream of tartar until soft
peaks form. Using a rubber spatula, gently fold half the egg
whites into the batter until almost fully incorporated. Add the
remaining egg whites and gently fold them in until just combined,
being careful to not overmix. Divide the batter evenly among the
prepared pans.

Bake until a toothpick inserted in the center comes out clean,
22 to 25 minutes. Turn the layers out onto a wire rack and allow
them to cool completely.

To make the whipped cream: In a chilled bowl, combine the cream,
powdered sugar, honey, and rose water. Using a chilled whisk, whip
by hand or with an electric mixer until soft peaks form.

To assemble the cake: Place one layer on a cake plate and dollop
whipped cream on top. Repeat with the next layer. Top the cake
with the remaining layer and spread more whipped cream on top;
sprinkle with the pistachios and orange zest.

Blood Orange
OLIVE OIL CAKE

SERVES 8

Blood oranges are so dramatic, with scarlet interiors and blushing skins, and I love their bittersweet flavor. That tartness plays well off the bold flavor of the olive oil in this cake.

Preheat the oven to 350°F (175°C). Butter a 9-inch (23-cm) round cake pan.

Melt the butter in a small saucepan over medium heat, then add the brown sugar and stir until dissolved. Pour the mixture into the prepared pan and arrange the orange slices on top.

In a small bowl, whisk together the sugar, eggs, oil, vanilla, and orange juice and zest.

In a large mixing bowl, whisk the together flour, baking powder, baking soda, and salt. Pour the oil mixture into the flour mixture, stirring until just combined.

Spread the batter over the oranges and bake until a toothpick inserted in the center comes out clean, about 30 minutes.

Let the cake cool in the pan for 15 minutes, then invert it onto a plate.

4 tablespoons (55 g) unsalted butter

¾ cup (165 g) packed light brown sugar

2 blood oranges, peeled and thinly sliced

1 cup (200 g) granulated sugar

2 large eggs

½ cup (120 ml) extra-virgin olive oil

1 teaspoon vanilla extract

Juice and zest of 1 blood orange

1½ cups (170 g) all-purpose flour

1 teaspoon baking powder

½ teaspoon baking soda

½ teaspoon salt

Candied Kumquat &

COCONUT CAKE

SERVES 8

This cake was born out of my overzealous purchasing of kumquats. I made a big batch of marmalade and still had some left over so I candied them and threw them on top of my favorite coconut cake.

For the candied kumquats:

1 cup (200 g) granulated sugar
1½ cups (200 g) kumquats, cut in half and seeded

For the cake:

2 cups (255 g) all-purpose flour
1 cup (200 g) granulated sugar
1 teaspoon baking powder
1 teaspoon baking soda
½ teaspoon salt
2 large eggs
1 cup (240 ml) whole milk
1 teaspoon vanilla extract
½ cup (1 stick/115 g) unsalted butter, melted
Zest of 1 orange
1 cup (90 g) sweetened shredded coconut

For the coconut flakes and whipped cream:

½ cup (40 g) unsweetened flaked coconut
1 (13.5-ounce/400-ml) can full-fat coconut milk, refrigerated overnight
2 tablespoons powdered sugar
½ teaspoon vanilla extract

To make the candied kumquats: In a medium saucepan, combine the sugar and 1 cup (240 ml) water and bring the mixture to a boil over medium-high heat, stirring until the sugar dissolves. Add the kumquats. Reduce the heat to medium-low and allow the mixture to simmer until the kumquats are soft and translucent, 10 to 15 minutes. Remove from the heat, strain off the liquid, and set the kumquats aside to cool.

To make the cake: Preheat the oven to 350°F (175°C). Butter a 10-inch (25-cm) round cake pan.

In a large bowl, whisk together the flour, sugar, baking powder, baking soda, and salt.

In a small bowl, whisk together the eggs, milk, and vanilla. Pour the egg mixture and the butter into the flour mixture, stirring until combined. Mix in the orange zest, coconut, and 1 cup (200 g) of the candied kumquats.

Pour the batter into the pan and bake until a toothpick inserted in the center comes out clean, 40 to 45 minutes. Allow the cake to cool in the pan for 10 minutes before turning it out onto a wire rack.

To make the coconut flakes and whipped cream: Spread the coconut in a single layer on a baking sheet and toast it in the oven alongside the cake until lightly browned, 5 to 6 minutes. Be sure to keep an eye on the coconut, as it will burn quickly.

Open the can of coconut milk and scoop out the firm layer of cream at the top (save the milk for another use). Place the cream into the bowl of an electric mixer fitted with the whisk attachment. Whip the cream until it becomes light and fluffy, 3 to 5 minutes. Mix in the powdered sugar and vanilla.

Top the cake with the whipped cream, toasted coconut flakes, and the remaining candied kumquats.

Cranberry
GINGERBREAD CAKE
SERVES 10

This is a grown-up Christmas cake. The molasses and coffee bring bitterness, and the ginger makes it spicy. I prefer dark molasses, but if you don't like that deep flavor, a lighter variety will be fine here.

This cake is a bit stubborn and sometimes sticks to the pan, so you can bake it in a parchment-lined 9-by-13-inch (23-by-33-cm) baking pan instead of the Bundt (although it's so good, I don't mind eating it directly out of the pan if it falls apart).

1 cup (240 ml) strong brewed coffee

1 cup (240 ml) dark unsulfured molasses

½ teaspoon baking soda

2¼ cups (285 g) all-purpose flour

½ teaspoon salt

1½ teaspoons baking powder

1 tablespoon ground ginger

1½ teaspoons ground cinnamon

½ teaspoon freshly grated nutmeg

¼ teaspoon ground cloves

¾ cup (180 ml) vegetable oil

3 large eggs

2 cups (440 g) packed dark brown sugar

1 cup (115 g) fresh cranberries, plus more for garnishing

Powdered sugar, for dusting

Preheat the oven to 350°F (175°C). Butter a 10-inch (25-cm) Bundt pan.

In a large saucepan, combine the coffee and molasses, bring the mixture to a boil over medium-high heat, then remove the pan from the heat. Whisk in the baking soda (the mixture will foam). Allow the syrup to cool.

In a medium bowl, whisk together the flour, salt, baking powder, ginger, cinnamon, nutmeg, and cloves.

In a large bowl, whisk together the oil, eggs, sugar, and molasses mixture. Add the flour mixture and stir until just combined. Stir in the cranberries.

Pour the batter into the pan. Bake until a tester inserted in the center comes out clean, about 50 minutes. Allow the cake to cool in the pan for 10 minutes, then invert it onto a wire rack and allow it to cool completely. Dust with powdered sugar and garnish with cranberries before serving.

Cranberry
GINGER CHEESECAKE

SERVES 8

This cheesecake would be a wonderful addition to any holiday table. The spicy ginger base topped with a sweet-tart cranberry sauce sings of holiday cheer!

For the topping: In a medium saucepan, combine the sugar with 1 cup (240 ml) water and bring the mixture to a boil over medium-high heat, stirring until the sugar has dissolved. Add the cranberries, reduce the heat to medium-low, and simmer until the berries burst, about 10 minutes. Stir in the ginger, remove from the heat, and allow the mixture to cool.

For the crust: Preheat the oven to 350°F (175°C). Butter a 9-inch (23-cm) springform pan.

Combine the gingersnap crumbs, sugar, butter, and salt. Press the mixture evenly into the prepared pan. Bake until the crust is crisp, 10 to 12 minutes. Leave the oven on.

For the filling: In a food processor, pulse the brown sugar and crystallized ginger until the ginger is very finely chopped.

In the bowl of an electric mixer fitted with the paddle attachment, beat the cream cheese and ginger-sugar mixture until smooth. Add the eggs and vanilla and mix until combined. Stir in the fresh ginger.

Pour the filling into the crust and bake for 45 minutes, or until the edges are set and the center moves only slightly when you shake it.

Transfer the pan to a wire rack and allow the cake to cool to room temperature before placing it in the refrigerator. Once the cheesecake is cool, remove it from the springform pan, top it with cranberry sauce, and sprinkle it with orange zest.

For the topping:
1 cup (200 g) granulated sugar
3 cups (345 g) fresh cranberries
1 tablespoon finely grated fresh ginger

For the crust:
1½ cups (130 g) gingersnap crumbs (from about 25 cookies)
2 tablespoons granulated sugar
4 tablespoons (55 g) unsalted butter, melted
Pinch of salt

For the filling and assembly:
1 cup (220 g) packed light brown sugar
¼ cup (35 g) finely chopped crystallized ginger
3 (8-ounce/226-g) packages cream cheese, softened
3 large eggs, room temperature
1 teaspoon vanilla extract
2 tablespoons finely grated fresh ginger
Zest of 1 orange, for sprinkling

DARK CHOCOLATE FLOURLESS CAKE

with Pomegranate Ganache

SERVES 8

People love this cake. I mean, really love it. It's
the one I take to parties that gets people begging me
for the recipe. It's deep and sweet, but it's also a
bit tangy from the pomegranate.

For the cake:

**8 ounces (225 g) dark
chocolate, chopped**

**½ cup (1 stick/115 g) unsalted
butter**

1 cup (200 g) granulated sugar

¼ teaspoon salt

1 teaspoon vanilla extract

4 large eggs

**½ cup (40 g) unsweetened cocoa
powder**

For the ganache and assembly:

**8 ounces (225 g) dark
chocolate, chopped**

½ cup (120 ml) heavy cream

**½ cup (120 ml) pomegranate
juice**

**1 cup (115 g) pomegranate
seeds**

To make the cake: Preheat the oven to 350°F (175°C). Butter a
9-inch (23-cm) springform pan.

In a medium saucepan, warm the chocolate and butter over
medium heat until they are just melted. Transfer the mixture to a
medium bowl and stir in the sugar, salt, and vanilla. Let cool.

Whisk in the eggs one at a time, beating until smooth. Add the
cocoa powder and stir to combine.

Pour the batter into the prepared pan and bake until set,
30 to 35 minutes. Let cool in the pan for 30 minutes. Run a knife
around the edge of the cake before unmolding it.

To make the ganache: Place the chocolate in a medium heatproof
bowl.

Pour the cream and pomegranate juice into a small saucepan
and bring the mixture to a boil over medium-high heat. Pour it over
the chocolate and let it stand for 5 minutes. Whisk until smooth.

To assemble the cake: Pour the ganache over the top of the cake
and sprinkle it with the pomegranate seeds.

Cranberry
ORANGE CAKE

This cake is so simple, but so buttery, rich, and flavorful. The eggs act as the leavening agent, so be sure to beat them well.

3 large eggs
2 cups (400 g) granulated sugar
¾ cup (1½ sticks/170 g) unsalted butter, room temperature
1 teaspoon vanilla extract
Zest of 1 orange
2 cups (255 g) all-purpose flour
½ teaspoon ground cloves
8 ounces (225 g) fresh cranberries

Preheat the oven to 350°F (175°C). Butter a 9-by-13-inch (23-by-33-cm) baking pan.

In the bowl of an electric mixer fitted with the paddle attachment, beat the eggs and sugar until the mixture thickens slightly and turns light in color, 3 to 5 minutes. Add the butter, vanilla, and orange zest and beat for another 2 minutes. Add the flour and cloves, stirring until just combined. Stir in the cranberries.

Spread the batter evenly into the prepared pan. Bake for 40 to 45 minutes, until a toothpick inserted in the center comes out clean. Allow the cake to cool completely in the pan.

Meyer Lemon
LAVENDER CAKE

SERVES 8

I vividly remember the first time I tried lavender. I was at a dinner party far too fancy for my eighteen-year-old self, and at the end of the meal, the server set a lemon-lavender sorbet in front of me. I was a bit worried, but when I tried a bite, I loved it. Since then, the combination of lemon and lavender has stuck with me. I like using Meyer lemons especially, as their floral notes meld so well with the lavender flavor.

To make the cake: Preheat the oven to 350°F (175°C). Butter a 10-inch (25-cm) Bundt pan.

In a medium bowl, whisk together the flour, baking powder, baking soda, salt, and lavender.

In a small bowl, combine the milk, lemon zest and juice, and vanilla (the milk will curdle from the lemon juice—that's totally fine!).

In the bowl of an electric mixer fitted with the paddle attachment, cream the butter and sugar until light and fluffy, 3 to 5 minutes. Add the eggs one at a time, scraping down the sides of the bowl after each addition. Alternate adding the flour mixture and the milk mixture to the mixer bowl, beginning and ending with the flour.

Pour the batter into the prepared pan and bake until a tester inserted in the center comes out clean, 50 to 55 minutes. Allow the cake to cool slightly in the pan.

To make the glaze: In a medium bowl, whisk together the powdered sugar and lemon juice. Pour the glaze over the warm cake.

For the cake:

3 cups (385 g) all-purpose flour
1 teaspoon baking powder
1 teaspoon baking soda
1 teaspoon salt
1 teaspoon dried lavender
¾ cup (180 ml) whole milk
Zest and juice of 4 Meyer lemons
1 teaspoon vanilla extract
1 cup (2 sticks/225 g) unsalted butter, room temperature
2 cups (400 g) granulated sugar
4 large eggs

For the glaze:

1 cup (100 g) powdered sugar
3 to 4 tablespoons (45 to 60 ml) Meyer lemon juice

PEAR & ALMOND CHOCOLATE CAKE

with Cider Glaze

SERVES 10

The cider used here is not of the alcoholic variety, but rather, unfiltered juice. If you can't get your hands on pear cider, apple cider would work well too.

For the cake:

1 cup (240 ml) boiling water

½ cup (40 g) unsweetened cocoa powder

2 cups (255 g) all-purpose flour

2 teaspoons baking powder

2 teaspoons ground cardamom

1 teaspoon salt

2 cups (440 g) packed light brown sugar

1 cup (240 ml) vegetable oil

2 teaspoons vanilla extract

2 large eggs

2 pears, peeled, cored, and diced into ¼-inch (6-mm) pieces

½ cup (55 g) slivered almonds

For the glaze:

1 cup (240 ml) pear cider

3 tablespoons packed light brown sugar

2 tablespoons unsalted butter

½ teaspoon ground cinnamon or cardamom

Powdered sugar, for dusting

To make the cake: Preheat the oven to 350°F (175°C). Butter a 10-inch (25-cm) tube pan.

In a medium bowl, whisk together the boiling water and cocoa powder. Allow the mixture to cool.

In a large bowl, combine the flour, baking powder, cardamom, and salt.

In the bowl of an electric mixer fitted with the whisk attachment, combine the brown sugar, oil, and vanilla. Add the eggs one at a time, scraping down the sides of the bowl after each addition.

Beat in half of the flour mixture, then the cocoa mixture. Add the remaining flour mixture. Stir in the pears and almonds.

Transfer the batter to the prepared pan and bake until a tester inserted in the center comes out clean, about 1 hour. Allow the cake to cool in the pan for 10 minutes, then turn it out onto a wire rack to cool completely.

To make the glaze: In a small saucepan, stir together the cider, brown sugar, butter, and cinnamon or cardamom. Bring the mixture to a boil over medium-high heat. Reduce the heat to medium-low and allow the mixture to simmer until it has thickened slightly. Pour the glaze over the cake and dust with powdered sugar.

Meyer Lemon & Thyme
CHIFFON CAKE

SERVES 10

This cake is light and airy like an angel food cake, but richer because of the egg yolks and oil. The minty, earthy flavor of the thyme complements the tang and sweetness of the Meyer lemon perfectly.

To make the cake: Preheat the oven to 325°F (165°C). Set aside an ungreased 10-inch (25-cm) tube pan with a removable bottom.

In a large bowl, whisk together the flour, sugar, baking powder, and salt.

In a medium bowl, whisk together the oil, egg yolks, lemon zest and juice, and ½ cup (120 ml) water. Add the liquid mixture to the flour mixture and stir until just combined.

In the bowl of an electric mixer fitted with the whisk attachment, beat the egg whites and cream of tartar until stiff peaks form. Using a rubber spatula, gently fold half the egg whites into the batter until they are almost fully incorporated. Add the remaining egg whites and gently fold until just combined, being careful to not overmix.

Pour the batter into the pan and bake until a tester inserted in the center comes out clean, 45 to 50 minutes. Immediately invert the pan onto a wire rack and allow the cake to cool completely while upside down in the pan.

Gently tap the pan until the cake comes out.

To make the glaze: While the cake is cooling, whisk together the powdered sugar and lemon juice in a medium bowl. Add about 2 tablespoons water to reach the desired consistency—it should be thick but pourable. Whisk in the thyme leaves. Pour the glaze over the cake.

For the cake:
2¼ cups (315 g) cake flour
1½ cups (300 g) granulated sugar
1 tablespoon baking powder
½ teaspoon salt
½ cup (120 ml) vegetable oil
7 large eggs, separated
Zest and juice of 3 or 4 Meyer lemons (enough for ½ cup/120 ml juice)
½ teaspoon cream of tartar

For the glaze:
1¼ cups (125 g) powdered sugar
Juice of 1 Meyer lemon
2 teaspoons fresh thyme leaves

LEMON CAKE

with Black Tea Frosting

SERVES 8

This is an Arnold Palmer in cake form, with tart
lemon layers and a black tea–infused frosting.

For the cake:

1⅔ cups (215 g) all-purpose
  flour
2 teaspoons baking powder
1 teaspoon salt
½ cup (1 stick/115 g) unsalted
  butter, room temperature
1 cup (200 g) granulated sugar
Zest of 2 lemons
3 large eggs
1 cup (240 ml) buttermilk
1 teaspoon vanilla extract
½ teaspoon lemon extract

For the frosting:

3 large egg whites
¼ teaspoon cream of tartar
¾ cup (150 g) granulated sugar
⅔ cup (165 ml) strong brewed
  black tea

To make the cake: Preheat the oven to 350°F (175°C). Butter two 6-inch (15-cm) round cake pans and line the bottom of each pan with parchment.

In a medium bowl, whisk together the flour, baking powder, and salt.

In the bowl of an electric mixer fitted with the paddle attachment, beat the butter, sugar, and lemon zest until the mixture is light and fluffy, 3 to 5 minutes. Add the eggs one at a time, scraping down the sides of the bowl after each addition.

In a bowl, combine the buttermilk, vanilla, and lemon extract.

Alternate adding the flour mixture and the buttermilk mixture to the mixing bowl, beginning and ending with the flour.

Divide the batter evenly between the prepared pans. Bake for 25 to 30 minutes, until a toothpick inserted in the center comes out clean. Allow the layers to cool for 10 minutes in the pans before turning them out onto a wire rack to cool completely.

To make the frosting: In the bowl of an electric mixer fitted with the whisk attachment, whip the egg whites and cream of tartar until stiff peaks form.

In a small saucepan, combine the sugar and half of the black tea. Bring the mixture to a boil over medium-high heat and cook, without stirring, until a candy thermometer immersed in the syrup reads 248°F (120°C).

Begin beating the egg whites again and slowly pour the boiling tea syrup in a slow stream into the bowl. Beat until stiff peaks have formed and the frosting has cooled.

Add the remaining black tea by the tablespoon, beating well.

To assemble the cake: Place one cake layer on a plate, and spread the top with frosting. Add the remaining layer and frost the outside of the cake.

Grapefruit Curd–Glazed
CITRUS CUPCAKES

MAKES 12

These little cakes pack a powerful citrus punch! I like to top mine with a slice of blood orange, but any citrus will do.

To make the cupcakes: Preheat the oven to 350°F (175°C). Line a cupcake pan with paper liners.

In a medium bowl, whisk together the all-purpose flour, cake flour, baking powder, and salt.

In the bowl of an electric mixer fitted with the paddle attachment, cream the butter and sugar until light and fluffy, 3 to 5 minutes. Add the eggs one at a time, scraping down the sides of the bowl after each addition. Beat in the lemon, lime, and orange zests. Alternate adding the flour mixture and the milk to the mixer bowl, beginning and ending with the flour.

Divide the batter evenly among the paper liners, filling each two-thirds full. Bake for 17 to 20 minutes, until a toothpick inserted in the center comes out clean.

Turn out onto a wire rack and allow the cupcakes to cool completely.

To make the curd and assemble: While the cupcakes are cooling, in a medium saucepan, whisk together the eggs, egg yolks, grapefruit juice, sugar, and salt. Heat over medium, whisking constantly, until the mixture is thick enough to coat the back of a spoon, 5 to 7 minutes.

Remove the saucepan from the heat and add the butter, one piece at a time, stirring until smooth. Allow the curd to cool slightly. Top each cupcake with cooled curd and a citrus slice.

For the cupcakes:
1 cup (130 g) all-purpose flour
1 cup (140 g) cake flour
1½ teaspoons baking powder
¼ teaspoon salt
½ cup (1 stick/115 g) unsalted butter, room temperature
1 cup (200 g) granulated sugar
2 large eggs
Zest of 1 lemon
Zest of 1 lime
Zest of 1 orange
½ cup (120 ml) whole milk

For the curd and assembly:
2 large eggs
2 large egg yolks
½ cup (120 ml) freshly squeezed grapefruit juice
½ cup (100 g) granulated sugar
Pinch of salt
4 tablespoons (55 g) unsalted butter, cubed
Citrus slices, for topping

Lemon-Rosemary
CUSTARD CAKE

SERVES 8

This is one of those magical baking tricks that invokes stares of disbelief. You start with a very thin batter and end with a layer of custard topped with a layer of cake. It's crazy, and delicious. Make sure the milk is lukewarm; otherwise, the butter will solidify.

¾ cup (90 g) all-purpose flour
¾ cup (150 g) granulated sugar
¼ teaspoon salt
4 large eggs, separated
½ cup (1 stick/115 g) unsalted butter, melted and cooled
2 cups (480 ml) milk, room temperature
¼ cup (60 ml) lemon juice
Zest of 1 lemon
1 tablespoon finely chopped fresh rosemary
Powdered sugar, for dusting

Preheat the oven to 350°F (175°C). Butter an 8-inch (20-cm) square baking pan.

In a large bowl, whisk together the flour, sugar, and salt.

In a medium bowl, whisk together the egg yolks and butter until well blended. Whisk in the milk, lemon juice, lemon zest, and rosemary. Whisk the lemon mixture into the flour mixture.

In the bowl of an electric mixer fitted with the whisk attachment, beat the egg whites until stiff peaks form. Gently fold the whites into the lemon mixture and pour the batter into the prepared pan. Bake for 45 minutes, or until golden brown.

Allow the cake to cool completely in the pan and dust with powdered sugar before serving.

Minty Grapefruit
PAVLOVA

SERVES 6

Most people think summer berries when they think pavlova, but it's delicious with tart citrus, too.

For the topping and assembly:
1 cup (40 g) fresh mint leaves, roughly chopped, plus more for garnishing
1 cup (200 g) granulated sugar
2 large Ruby Red grapefruits, peeled and sliced thinly

For the pavlova:
4 large egg whites, room temperature
½ teaspoon cream of tartar
Pinch of salt
1 teaspoon vanilla extract
1 cup (200 g) granulated sugar

For the whipped cream:
1 cup (240 ml) heavy cream
2 tablespoons powdered sugar

To make the topping: Place the mint in a medium heatproof bowl.

In a small saucepan, combine the sugar and 1 cup (240 ml) water. Heat over medium-high, stirring, until the sugar dissolves. Bring the syrup to a boil. Reduce the heat to medium-low and let it simmer for 3 minutes.

Pour the sugar syrup over the mint. Cover the bowl with plastic wrap and let the syrup steep for at least an hour or overnight.

Place the grapefruit in a medium bowl and pour the syrup over it through a fine-mesh sieve. Discard the mint. Refrigerate the grapefruit for 2 hours.

To make the pavlova: Preheat the oven to 275°F (135°C). Line a baking sheet with parchment paper. Trace a 9-inch (23-cm) circle on the parchment, using a cake pan as a guide. Flip the parchment over.

In the bowl of an electric mixer fitted with the whisk attachment, beat the egg whites, cream of tartar, and salt at a medium-low speed until soft peaks form. Stir in the vanilla.

Gradually add half of the sugar and increase the speed to medium-high, beating until the meringue holds stiff, glossy peaks.

Add the remaining sugar and beat until very stiff peaks form.

Using a spatula, mound the meringue onto the parchment circle. Spread it into a round, using the circle as a guide.

Put the baking sheet in the oven and immediately reduce the temperature to 250°F (120°C). Bake the meringue for 1 hour, or until it is dry to the touch and sounds hollow when tapped. Turn off the oven and leave the pavlova inside, allowing it to cool completely.

To make the whipped cream: Combine the cream and powdered sugar in a chilled bowl and, using a chilled whisk, whip by hand or with an electric mixer until soft peaks form.

To assemble the pavlova: Spread the cooked pavlova with whipped cream, arrange the grapefruit on top, and garnish it with mint.

Orange-Clove
POLENTA CAKE

SERVES 8

Each Christmas, my sister and I get together and make clove-studded orange pomanders. This cake is inspired by those pomanders, and it smells exactly like my house during the holidays.

To make the cake: Preheat the oven to 350°F (175°C). Butter an 8-inch (20-cm) square baking pan.

In a medium bowl, whisk together the polenta, almond flour, baking powder, and cloves.

In the bowl of an electric mixer fitted with the paddle attachment, cream the butter and sugar until light and fluffy, 3 to 5 minutes. Add the eggs one at a time, scraping down the sides of the bowl after each addition. Add the orange zest and vanilla. Add the flour mixture, stirring until just combined.

Spread the batter into the prepared pan and bake for 35 to 40 minutes, until a toothpick inserted in the center comes out clean.

To make the glaze: While the cake is baking, in a small saucepan, combine the honey with the orange juice and bring the mixture to a simmer over medium heat.

When the cake comes out of the oven, poke holes in the top using a wooden skewer or fork. Pour the glaze over the cake and allow it to soak in. Sprinkle the orange zest on top. Allow the cake to cool completely in the pan.

For the cake:
¾ cup (105 g) polenta (medium or coarsely ground cornmeal)
2 cups (280 g) almond flour
2 teaspoons baking powder
½ teaspoon ground cloves
1 cup (2 sticks/225 g) unsalted butter, room temperature
1 cup (200 g) granulated sugar
2 large eggs
Zest of 2 large oranges
1 teaspoon vanilla extract

For the glaze:
¼ cup (60 ml) honey
Juice and zest of 1 orange

SPICED PARSNIP CAKE

with Toasted Walnut–Brown Sugar Glaze

SERVES 10

> It's a shame that carrots get all the love when it comes to baking with root vegetables, as parsnips give such a lovely, sweet earthiness. You can even make this a day ahead—the flavors only get better with time.

To make the cake: Preheat the oven to 350°F (175°C). Butter a 9-by-13-inch (23-by-33-cm) baking pan.

In a medium bowl, whisk together the flour, baking powder, baking soda, cinnamon, ginger, nutmeg, allspice, cloves, and salt.

In a large bowl, whisk together the brown sugar, oil, and yogurt until well blended. Whisk in the eggs one at a time. Add the flour mixture and stir until blended. Stir in the parsnips.

Pour the batter into the prepared pan and bake for 40 to 45 minutes, until a toothpick inserted in the center comes out clean.

To make the glaze: While the cake is baking, spread the walnuts in a single layer in a baking pan and toast them in the oven alongside the cake just until they become aromatic, about 6 minutes. Roughly chop.

In a small saucepan, combine the brown sugar, butter, cream, and vanilla. Cook the mixture over medium heat until the sugar dissolves and the syrup thickens slightly. Whisk until smooth. Remove the pan from the heat and add the walnuts. Pour the glaze over the warm cake. Allow the cake to cool completely in the pan.

For the cake:

2 cups (255 g) all-purpose flour
1 teaspoon baking powder
1 teaspoon baking soda
2 teaspoons ground cinnamon
1 teaspoon ground ginger
¼ teaspoon freshly grated nutmeg
½ teaspoon ground allspice
¼ teaspoon ground cloves
½ teaspoon salt
1½ cups (330 g) packed light brown sugar
¾ cup (180 ml) vegetable oil
½ cup (120 ml) plain full-fat yogurt
3 large eggs
2 cups (220 g) peeled and grated parsnips

For the glaze:

1 cup (100 g) walnuts
½ cup (110 g) packed dark brown sugar
4 tablespoons (55 g) unsalted butter
¼ cup (60 ml) heavy cream
½ teaspoon vanilla extract

ACKNOWLEDGMENTS

Without the good people in my life, this book wouldn't have been possible.
I'd like to give the following thanks:

To my parents, for their love, guidance, and support in all my endeavors. Thank you so much for letting me make my own path and always being my cheerleaders, no matter what. To my sister, Sarah, for being my sous chef, model, and best friend. To my brother, Hayden, for keeping me laughing and always asking if the sweets have been photographed before taking a bite. To Bethany Anderson, for your friendship and undying love of strawberry-basil buttercream. To DeGina Scoggins, for helping me find my way in the kitchen with all those crazy catering jobs. To Ande Cook, for being my most enthusiastic supporter and always giving me advice when I need it. To all the *Honey & Jam* readers, for visiting my little corner of the Internet and for helping to turn my dreams into reality. And lastly, to the Avett Brothers, for providing the best cookbook-writing soundtrack a girl could ask for.

With love, Hannah

INDEX

Page numbers in *italics* refer to photographs.

Roasted Kabocha Squash Cinnamon
   Roll Cake with Sage–Maple Glaze,
   172–73
rolls, cake, 84, *154*, 155, 172–73
rosemary, 30
     Apple Skillet Cake with Rosemary
        Crumble, 146, *147*
     Lemon–Rosemary Custard Cake,
        212, *213*
     Rosemary Cornmeal Pound Cake
        with Caramelized Plums, *122*, 123
     Rosemary Crumble, 146, *147*
rosette frosting technique, 53
rose water, 184

S

sage, 30, 166, 172–73
Sage–Maple Glaze, 172–73
salt, 41, 47
Salted Caramel Cream, *154*, 155
Savory Spinach Cake, *86*, 87
scales (measuring), 47
self-rising flours, 41, 56
     See also flours
shortcakes, 66, *67*, *136*, 137
sieves, 44
sifters, 44
soft white winter wheat flours, 40–41
spatulas, 45, 48, 53
Spiced Parsnip Cake with Toasted
   Walnut–Brown Sugar Glaze, *216*, 217
Spiced Pumpkin Cupcakes with
   Bourbon Buttercream, 156, *157*
spinach, 87
spring produce, 16, *17*, 18
     *See also specific spring produce by
        name*
squashes
     fall, 29–30, 167, 172–73
     storage of, 22, 25, 30
     summer, 22, 25, 134
staples, pantry, 37, 38, *39*, 40–41
storage
     of fall fruits and vegetables, 29, 30,
        31
     of herbs, 30
     of spring fruits and vegetables, 16, 18
     of summer fruits and vegetables, 19,
        20, 22, 23, 25, 26
     of winter fruits and vegetables, 33,
        34, 35

strawberries, 16, *17*
     Black Pepper–Roasted Strawberry
        Buttermilk Cake, 60, *61*
     Frozen Strawberry Cheesecake,
        64, 65
     Strawberry–Basil Buttercream, *58*,
        59
     Strawberry Layer Cake with
        Strawberry–Basil Buttercream,
        58, 59
     Strawberry–Mint Shortcakes, 66, *67*
     Strawberry–Rhubarb Victoria
        Sponge, 56, *57*
sugar, 38
     brown sugars, 38, 47, *216*, 217
     creaming, 47–48
     measuring, 47
     See also honey; maple syrup;
        molasses
summer produce, 19–20, *21*, 22–23, *24*,
     25–26, *27*, 134
     *See also specific summer produce
        by name*
Summer Squash & Banana Cake, 134,
     135
summer squashes, 22, 25, 134
supplies, 37, 42, *43*, 44–45
     See also supplies by name
sweeteners. *See* sugar
Sweet Potato Caramel Sauce, 160
sweet potatoes, 31
     Pumpkin Crepe Cake with
        Sweet Potato Caramel Sauce,
        160–61
     Sweet Potato Cupcakes with
        Marshmallow Frosting, *164*, 165
     Sweet Potato Sage Cake with Maple
        Glaze, 166
     Sweet Potato Whoopie Pies with
        Molasses Filling, 170, *171*
swirl frosting technique, 53

T

techniques, baking, 37, 47–48, 50–53
     *See also specific baking techniques
        by name*
tender herbs, 30
thermometers, 45
thyme, 30, *94*, 95, 137, *204*, 205
Toasted Walnut–Brown Sugar Glaze,
     216, 217

tomatoes, 22, 23, 25
     Green Tomato Cornmeal Cake, *118*,
        119
     Heirloom Tomato Cake, 113
     Peach & Tomato Preserves Cake,
        116, *117*
tortes, 179
tres leches cakes, *102*, 103
trifles, 92, *93*

U

upside-down cakes
     Dark Sweet Cherry Upside-Down
        Cake, *72*, 73
     Green Tomato Cornmeal Cake, *118*,
        119
     Plum & Apricot Upside-Down Cake,
        139
utensils, 44–45

V

Vanilla–Rhubarb jam, *78*, 79
vegetable and fruit peelers, 44

W

Walnut–Brown Sugar Glaze, *216*, 217
walnuts, 167, 217
wheat flours, 40–41
whipped cream, 48, 56, *57*, 66, *67*, 92,
     93, 100, *101*, *102*, 103, *106*, 107, *150*,
     151, 152, 184, *185*, 188, *189*, 214
whipping, cream and egg whites, 48
Whiskey, Pear & Maple Cheesecake, 178
White Lily flour, 40–41
white winter wheat flours, 40–41
whole wheat flours, 41
whoopie pies, 170, *171*
winter produce, *32*, 33–35
     *See also specific winter produce by
        name*
wire racks, 45
woody herbs, 30

Z

zucchini, 25, 133
Zucchini Chocolate Cake with Dark
   Chocolate Ganache, *132*, 133